"*The Art of Self-Compassion* is a tender and powerful guide that exposes shame as an impostor language. Through the surprisingly powerful practice of self-portraiture, Joy Prouty offers us an alternative dialect that feels like freedom and sounds like home. This book is a necessary companion for anyone ready to rewrite their inner narrative with compassion at its core."

    EMILY P. FREEMAN, *New York Times* bestselling author of *How to Walk into a Room*

"Joy Prouty knows the secret we're afraid to admit: We're all starving for permission to love ourselves exactly as we are—wonderfully flawed and achingly human. Offering the revolutionary idea that there's no way to get this wrong, she transforms the simple act of self-portraiture into a portal for healing the harsh voices in our heads. If you've ever worried your hand would be slapped for reaching for beauty and joy, let this be your invitation to reach anyway."

    MARY VAN GEFFEN, author of *Parenting a Spicy One: A Compassionate Guide for Raising a Deep-Feeling and Wonderfully Strong-Willed Kid*

"Joy Prouty's *The Art of Self-Compassion* is a soul-forming, luminous guide to healing the parts of ourselves we've long abandoned or feared. Through raw honesty, poetic insight, and humorous humility, Joy invites us to reclaim our stories, integrate our pain, and discover the quiet, revolutionary power of being gentle with ourselves."

    SCOTT ERICKSON, author of *Honest Advent* and *Say Yes*

"Joy Prouty's piercing yet gentle insight into how we can observe our human experience through a camera lens is a needed antidote in a world of AI-generated images and regurgitated clichés. By reinterpreting the power of photography as a window to our souls rather than a mirror for our egos, Joy releases us to unlearn our negativity bias and be moved by the beauty of our own lives. It's a pleasure to enter Joy's world, where her honest, natural poetry and moving images release us from the prison of self-criticism and open us to awe."

JULIE BOGART, author of *Raising Critical Thinkers* and founder of Brave Writer

"Amid a reality that often feels fragmented and surreal, we long for solace in what is real. In *The Art of Self-Compassion*, Joy Prouty is at her poetic, tender, visionary best, calling us to beauty and reminding us we're worthy. This book is a balm of sacred wholeness when we need it most."

SHANNAN MARTIN, author of *Start with Hello* and *The Ministry of Ordinary Places*

"Good photographers teach us to see the mystical in our world. Exceptional photographers teach us to see the mystical in ourselves. Through the pages of this book, Joy Prouty steps out from behind the camera to empower each of us with the gift of seeing—anytime, anywhere. The world will be a little softer because of it."

SHANNON K. EVANS, author of *The Mystics Would Like a Word* and *Rewilding Motherhood*

"*The Art of Self-Compassion* is a burning bush—tender, luminous, and fiercely true. With courage and grace, Joy Prouty invites us to see what we thought we could not: the beauty in our own becoming. These pages are not just about photography; they are an invitation to be undone by love and remade by grace."

TARA M. OWENS, CSD, CSDS, spiritual director, founder of Anam Cara Ministries, and author of *Embracing the Body: Finding God in Our Flesh and Bone*

THE ART OF
SELF-COMPASSION

Books by Joy Prouty

Practicing Presence
The Art of Self-Compassion

THE ART OF SELF-COMPASSION

HOW TO OFFER YOURSELF GENTLE ACCEPTANCE
AND RECLAIM YOUR WORTH

JOY PROUTY

BakerBooks
a division of Baker Publishing Group
Grand Rapids, Michigan

© 2026 by Joy Prouty

Published by Baker Books
a division of Baker Publishing Group
Grand Rapids, Michigan
BakerBooks.com

Printed in China

All rights reserved. No part of this publication may be reproduced, stored in a retrieval system, or transmitted in any form or by any means—for example, electronic, photocopy, recording—without the prior written permission of the publisher. The only exception is brief quotations in printed reviews.

Library of Congress Cataloging-in-Publication Control Number: 2025002676
ISBN 9781540904225 (cloth)
ISBN 9781493450374 (ebook)

Cover and interior photos by Joy Prouty
Endsheets and page 171 photos by Cere Demuth
Cover design by Chris Kuhatschek
Interior design by William Overbeeke

The author is represented by the literary agency of Punchline Agency, LLC, www.punchlineagency.com.

Baker Publishing Group publications use paper produced from sustainable forestry practices and postconsumer waste whenever possible.

26 27 28 29 30 31 32   7 6 5 4 3 2 1

For those who chase the light

CONTENTS

Foreword by K.J. Ramsey 13
A Letter to the Reader 17

PART ONE
HOW SELF-PORTRAITS HELP US LEARN TO SEE

1. Discovering a Perspective of Empathy 23
2. Answering the Call of Beauty 32
3. Contemplation That Leads to Transformation 53

PART TWO
LEARNING TO SEE ALL OF LIFE AS AN ART

4. Validating Emotion 71
5. Embodying Authenticity 88
6. Moving from Criticism to Curiosity 105
7. Claiming Wholeness 124
8. Releasing the Weight of Shame 143
9. Embracing Joy 162
10. Attuning to the Frequency of Love 177

Acknowledgments 199
Notes 203

The truth is always an abyss. One must—as in a swimming pool—dare to dive from the quivering springboard of trivial everyday experience and sink into the depths, in order to later rise again—laughing and fighting for breath—to the now doubly illuminated surface of things.

Franz Kafka

FOREWORD

The most beautiful people I have ever met are not the ones whose faces are perfectly symmetrical or free from wrinkles or acne or scars. The most beautiful people I have ever met are the ones who—just by being present—reveal the beauty you hadn't yet been able to see.

My friend Joy Prouty came to stay at my house for a few days last May, just as I was beginning to reemerge from a long and brutal season of life-threatening illness. The day Joy arrived, we sat for hours on my back deck in the bright Colorado sun, sipping sparkling waters and trading stories of what we each had survived in the previous year. To even be well enough to sit on my back deck for hours with a friend felt miraculous. But it also felt vulnerable to let a long-distance friend see how much my body had changed.

I was around fifty pounds heavier than the person Joy had previously known. High-dose steroids had kept me alive in the hospital and beyond, but they also rapidly heaped weight on my already curvy frame. At one point my face had swollen so much that my iPhone no longer recognized it as mine. By the time Joy visited, I was just starting to see my face as mine again. Sometimes I would see my reflection and the new jagged scars on my chest would still startle me.

As we caught up, Joy noticed the large shrub behind me in the corner of our yard, bursting with round white flowers. I told Joy that the viburnum had been in our yard before we moved there. Its name comes from the Latin for "wayfaring tree" because the plant spreads so easily through the birds who eat its fruit, carrying the seeds of its beauty from place to place. I had been watching its slow progression for months—from barren to budding, to small orbs of lime green, finally to that week's blizzard of snowballed blooms.

When Joy asked if she could photograph me with the viburnum, I said yes. I stood amid the blooms, letting the sun's golden light bathe my bare, scarred chest, letting my friend give me the chance to see myself in that moment as beautiful. Not the self I used to be nor the self I wished I could be again, but the self who was slowly recovering.

I later learned that viburnum not only symbolize new life and resilience but are seen as guardians against negativity. The images Joy and I made together that day have served as guardians of grace for me, reminding me to always look for the beauty in my own becoming.

Joy gave me the gift of seeing the sacred in what *is*.

The book you are about to read is a powerful invitation. Just as Joy invited me to stand in the light of the sun, she invites you to see the beauty of who you are and who you will become.

May the grace you encounter in this book give you courage to see your life as sacred, and may that sight become like seeds, spreading beauty everywhere you go.

K.J. Ramsey, licensed therapist and author
of *The Book of Common Courage*
March 29, 2025

A LETTER TO THE READER

This is a book about learning to love yourself using photography as a modality of healing.

Within these pages are stories gleaned from my years of work as a portrait artist documenting the whole spectrum of living for my clients—birth, death, and all the layers of transformation in between. It has been fascinating learning about human nature and the fears most of us carry when it comes to being seen; the camera can bring up a lot of tender, unexpected inner wounds.

Photographs are mirrors reflecting back to us everything we seek to hide, hope to embody, and pray we never forget.

My clients have been wise guides in my creative and spiritual expansion, and in observing them being brave, I felt courageous enough to begin using the camera as a therapeutic tool for preserving proof of my own healing journey. I photographed myself as I worked through facing my childhood trauma, as I deconstructed and reconstructed my faith, and as I reclaimed my original creative voice as inherently worthy and beloved.

Becoming a compassionately curious witness of my own life for the purpose of making art helped me to shift from a perspective of criticism and scarcity to one of acceptance and expanse.

The photographs I hope you create are not to be analyzed, obsessed over, or perfected to fit into any sort of category of "rightness," and they are not for putting on a Christmas card as a shiny projection that you've got it all together. They are for becoming present to your own power and for bearing empathetic witness to your multilayered experience of feeling and healing.

At the end of each chapter in part 2, you will find contemplative questions as well as self-portrait prompts. If you have a phone with a camera, I imagine you are already documenting your life in pictures. The goal now is to bring more intention and self-reflection into the photos you are already taking.

The following is a framework I have most recently used for bringing more intention into the portrait experience. I encourage you to use it as a guide for crafting a presence practice that feels authentic, nourishing, and practical for you in your own life.

CREATING IMAGES OF SELF-COMPASSION

1. **Embodiment.** Slow down, breathe, and turn toward yourself with gentleness. Instead of trying to make sense of things in your head, get into your actual senses.
2. **Validation.** Notice which emotions you feel. Name, validate, and embrace them without needing to understand or make sense of them. Let them be present and flow through you without judgment.

3. **Preservation.** Preserve proof of your choice to be present and connected. You showed up for yourself with intention rather than numbing or distracting—yes!
4. **Self-Reflection.** If you created a digital image, take a minute to breathe, and then observe it. Please don't believe any of the thoughts that may begin to flood your mind if they are negative—let them pass like clouds. Let this be an opportunity for tender curiosity. What offering of compassion can you give yourself in the moment?

Holding the tension of all our roles in life can feel at times like tightrope walking. When we don't have a point of focus, we can fall to the depths, taking everyone we love down with us.

By setting our focus on self-compassion and directing our attention toward all the love accessible from deep within ourselves—rather than seeking external validation from others—the portal to seeing life ripe with opportunities for art-making is revealed.

I hope this book becomes a companion. Know that I am right alongside you with my camera slung over my shoulder, good snacks in my backpack, and a little bit of wisdom in my pocket for us as we find our way through the valleys.

PART ONE

HOW SELF-PORTRAITS HELP US LEARN TO SEE

CHAPTER 1

DISCOVERING A PERSPECTIVE OF EMPATHY

> Compassion is not a virtue—it is a commitment. It's not something we have or don't have—it's something we choose to practice.
>
> Brené Brown

The image regarded as the most influential photograph in history was captured by astronaut William Anders in 1968 during the Apollo 8 mission. It was the first color photograph of Earth captured from space that humanity had ever seen.

In a televised interview that took place after the mission's return, Anders was asked how it felt to have captured the widely resonating image titled *Earthrise*. He pondered thoughtfully before sharing how his first instinct was that the space program really should have *sent a poet*.[1]

He was aware that no picture could possibly encompass how it felt to witness that moment in real time, yet he still scrambled to switch out his black-and-white film for a roll of color and at least attempt to preserve proof of his experience. I find it so fascinating that the intention of taking the camera on the Apollo 8 mission was to document a distant and unexplored foreign landscape, but it turned out the greatest impact was not in discovering something new but in gaining a fresh perspective on home.

The mind-blowing and compassion-inducing photograph has been credited with initiating the global environmental movement because it communicated without words how vulnerable and isolated Earth is—a beautiful blue marble floating in a dark abyss of ever-expanding unknowns. An article in *The New York Times* spoke about the impact of the image on our culture at the time, declaring that the "mission was viewed as briefly reviving the spirits of an America stunned by rising casualties in the Vietnam War, the assassinations of the Rev. Dr. Martin Luther King Jr. and Robert F. Kennedy, and tumultuous antiwar protests and racial disturbances."[2]

It was a *photograph* that ushered in a unified and empathetic perspective during a time of great hopelessness and sorrow.

This humbling and artistic view of our collective landscape made humanity undeniably aware of our fragility as individuals but also our strength as an interconnected whole. NASA administrator and former senator Bill Nelson said this about Anders: "He traveled to the threshold of the Moon and helped all of us see something else: ourselves."[3]

The journey of life does work this way, it seems—we think we are on one path and then, in an unexpected moment of clarity and presence, we realize our purpose is much greater and also simpler than we once perceived. Those moments of presence that we preserve in photographs are crucial; they serve as doors back into remembering our embodied awe.

> Those moments of presence that we preserve in photographs are crucial; they serve as doors back into remembering our embodied awe.

In an interview for *Forbes* in 2015, William Anders explained that he wasn't even supposed to have taken that photo—he was supposed to be saving the film to document specific moon craters only, as the number of rolls they could take into space was limited. He even shared about feeling guilty after photographing Earth because it wasn't part of their mission directive.[4]

I was surprised he mentioned feeling guilt, maybe because that is such a human response. I wasn't thinking about how this astronaut was just a person too, with all kinds of vulnerabilities. He had been up there to do a job and wondered if what he had spent the film on was, in fact, worthy of the cost.

I have often experienced that tender and exposed feeling of guilt after taking pictures of myself in moments of happiness. It is empowering in the moment to feel that level of awe, but then as time passes, negative self-talk can find its way in. There have been many times I've had to talk myself out of going back and deleting pictures after my anxiety has convinced me that taking photos of myself is embarrassing, just a self-absorbed waste of energy and camera roll storage space.

I learned about the *Earthrise* photograph on June 7, 2024, the day that astronaut William Anders died at the age of ninety. The iconic image he had taken was plastered across news outlets everywhere as they reported that the vintage T-34 plane Anders had been solo piloting accidentally crashed into the Salish Sea.

Coincidentally, an island in the Salish Sea is where I live, alongside my husband and our seven children. Since that tragic accident, I've learned from the locals that "Bill" was passionate and curious about exploration until his very last moment, and that he would regularly fly loops over the islands. I think, just maybe, the magic that called Bill Anders to join the space program and ultimately took him to the moon was the same magic that called him to the Salish Sea.

I have barely scratched the surface in knowing the history of this area, but what I have observed from my limited perspective is that no one comes to live on an island by accident. People come seeking safety, healing, and to reignite the elusive childlike spirit of wonder.

There is a rhythm of slowness and intentionality that touches every aspect of life on the island. It is only accessible by ferryboat or small chartered plane. Once on the island, there is not a single traffic light—only stop signs, a few roundabouts, and an abundance of unhurried people biking, walking, and admiring the natural beauty. Resident orca pods swim close to shore, as well as sea lions and the occasional breaching humpback whale. The island is widely covered in forest with a soft, vibrant, mossy green floor. Lush ferns create labyrinths beneath the massive, red-barked madrona trees, their trunks curving and dancing, reaching upward to the light. The island offers an immersion into and a relationship with the original essence of our planet.

This area mesmerizes me because I encountered very little time in the wild of nature while growing up. In fact, I spent very little time inhabiting my body; as much as possible, I lived life inside of my head. Growing up within the confines of a strict conservative church, I had absorbed the belief that my personal strength of will was to be subdued, and that my

thoughts, feelings, and curiosities about my body were sinful and wrong.

    I spent most of my childhood and teen years trying to make myself small and compliant in order to make sure that I would not lose the safety of social belonging. Perhaps that is why no matter how many years of talk therapy I did, I could never embody the emotional healing I was seeking until I immersed myself into nature as a *lifestyle*. It was then I realized: I am no different from this landscape. I am not superior to it, but I am one with it—ever-changing like the trees, the flowers, and the ocean tides. By seeing myself as one with nature, I found acceptance for myself in places I had previously held shame.

    Maybe after deconstructing all our untrue beliefs, the way we reconstruct hope is to become explorers within the abyss of our own darkness, like astronauts curiously marveling at outer space.

    What might happen if we could view the stories that we've been telling ourselves, the pain that we've been experiencing, and our resentment, anger, and sadness with compassionate curiosity instead of with criticism? Seeking not to judge and condemn but to witness with devotional honor. What if we invested our time and energy not in trying to numb our complexities but in discovering more creative ways of viewing ourselves through a lens of wonder and awe?

    Scientific research has proven that our bodies are made up of the very same elements as the galaxies, so who might we become if we artistically celebrated the expanse of our vibrant uniqueness rather than hiding beneath a facade of sameness?

    Photography has shifted since humanity first experienced *Earthrise* in 1968. I wish I could say that a new, mind-bending photograph of the heavens would have the same impact on our planet today, but advances in technology have changed our capacity for amazement. Very few of us still use analog film. Now we all carry digital cameras in our pockets to record memories. And with the rise of AI, there's the whole question of whether a photograph is even genuine, and we wonder how deeply the absence of authentic images will impact us.

We are caught in the dissonance between what is fake and what is real, not only in our photographs but also within our interior landscapes of identity.

As a professional photographer for over two decades, I have observed how the judgments we place upon our images in photographs closely reveal the deeper level of judgments we have for our true selves. The problem with this on a larger scale is that the unrealistic standards we attempt to hold ourselves to are the exact same unfair expectations we subconsciously place upon others.

The more focused we are on being perceived as flawless, the less capacity we have for empathy. By living unauthentically, we not only deprive ourselves of freedom but limit the freedom of true expression from those whose lives we touch.

I have used the practice of photographing myself to accompany my own emotional healing journey, and I have photographed others as a means of preserving proof of their identity expansion and spiritual growth. I believe that intentional art can be a portal to the image of God in us. We only must be willing to soften the harsh views we have of ourselves and open to receiving the loving awareness that we are each as baffling in beauty as the earth viewed from space.

Here's the thing . . . the world had seen the earth from space prior to the *Earthrise* image, but it had only been in black and white. It was the *color* of the image that brought expansive hope to humanity. The diverse and vibrant hues against the void of darkness was soul-shocking. So, on a personal level, what would it look like for us to zoom way out in our perception of self by releasing criticism, practicing healthy curiosity, and admiring the full spectrum of our colorful expanse with a posture of holy compassion?

The iconic photograph that Bill Anders captured while orbiting the moon changed the world because it forced people to confront the reality that none of us have, or ever will have, all the answers. Life is a mystery, and from a pulled-back perspective, all structures of religion fail to encompass the radiant magnitude of God. It is simply our inability to see *ourselves* as luminous that keeps us from attuning to the frequency of love.

Earthrise startled a sorrowful and disillusioned world into a posture of unexpected empathy—and that is exactly the kind of photographs I hope this book inspires you to create for the rarely seen and perhaps misunderstood parts deep inside of you.

Imagine me standing before you, swapping out your monochrome film for a fresh roll of color. What depths and details might be discovered through a more expansive and compassionate perspective?

CHAPTER 2

ANSWERING THE CALL OF BEAUTY

> In teaching us a new visual code, photographs alter and enlarge our notions of what is worth looking at and what we have a right to observe.
>
> Susan Sontag

With every photograph documented, we make the choice of what we will focus on, honor with our presence, and believe. Creating photographs of ourselves is a powerful way of tangibly rewriting the untrue stories unconsciously flowing within us.

In my decades of preserving images of people as a professional photographer, I have noticed over and over that when the camera comes out, most humans become anxious, fearful, and uncomfortable with the idea of having their picture made. Their breathing becomes shallow, their shoulders creep up to their ears in tension, and a pretend smile commonly appears on their faces. The images I have found that people tend to

dislike are not even ones where they look unattractive, per se, but those where they don't recognize the immobilized, less authentic versions of themselves.

I get it because I've felt it too—our culture and families of origin have often put us on the defensive when it comes to being seen. When we observe a reflection of ourselves in an image, our brains begin to instantly register all the stories we have told ourselves about our appearance and what other people might think about us. We hear the voices of criticism from our past, and of course there are all the marketing ploys that have presented us with impossible standards of perfection, which our brains then take as additional "evidence" that we will never measure up.

We were raised on a steady drip of societal pressure to fix ourselves, to cover all traces of authenticity and growth, and to buy more and more products to make ourselves look younger and untouched by wisdom and time. We have been sold the lie that change and growth are ugly and in need of fixing.

A woman whose writing has been a guide for me throughout my own journey of self-acceptance is spiritual mentor and author Liz Milani, who writes, "The grace of beauty is its breadth and depth of inclusivity."[1] We often think of inclusivity in regard to society and groups that are marginalized, but have you ever stopped to think that perhaps our culture's separation of who is "in" and who is "out" begins with the way we regard the less understood parts of ourselves?

Embracing the whole of who we are is the most loving thing we can do because we are no longer picking out which parts are worthy and which ones are not. Taking a posture of inclusivity brings forth beauty that is deep and transformative. We can't make an impact on the world or learn to love ourselves unconditionally if we are still shaming parts of ourselves or wishing them to be different. The journey of regaining self-worth not only benefits us individually but can heal us as a collective whole. Scientific research proves that having compassion for oneself inevitably leads to having compassion for others.

Self-compassion is, in fact, the farthest thing from selfishness.

A common belief in American culture is that being soft with ourselves is a downfall and a weakness. But according to Dr. Emma Seppala of Stanford University's Center for Compassion and Altruism Research and Education, the opposite is true. She writes,

> [Self-compassion] is actually the secret to resilience, strength in the face of failure, the ability to learn from mistakes and to bounce back with greater enthusiasm. Self-compassion involves treating oneself as one would a friend, being more mindful, and understanding our situation in the context of a larger human experience. When we can be more understanding and gentler with ourselves, identify less with the emotions that surround our mistakes, and understand that failure is a normal part of the larger human experience, we become stronger and more successful in the long run.[2]

The way we talk to and about our bodies reflects the way we talk to our inner child and to our soul. This is why the process of reinventing photos from childhood can be an incredibly therapeutic and empowering experience. I have done this for myself and for my photography clients.

I once photographed a woman seeking to redeem the power she remembered embodying in childhood. She had shared with me a photo from when she was three or four years old that she was hoping to re-create. She was standing on top of the coffee table in her childhood living room, wielding a scepter made of flowers and wearing a crown and a puffy, hot-pink princess gown. The look of conviction on her face was intense, and she told me she was "preaching" in the photo.

She believed this image depicted her real self who climbed up on tables and told people how she *really* felt. That power was still within her—she just needed a little help coaxing it out.

We met at a park and began by picking flowers to create a beautiful crown for her. She found a long branch covered in moss to be her scepter, and as we walked, we happened upon a picnic table for her to stand on to do some preaching. For the next few minutes, I just stood in awe of her courage. I created photographs of her moving to the rhythm of her most true self; it was an honor to witness what felt like a sacred experience of identity alignment. I saw her fiery childlikeness emerge as well as the maturity of her spiritual strength.

This photoshoot is an example of how becoming embodied for the purpose of photographs helps us learn the value of embodied *living*.

Growing up as a teenager in the '90s within purity culture in a strict, conservative church, I was taught that my body was a weapon of lust and must be concealed at all costs. I remember feeling like attuning to my body in any way was sinful and wrong. I was worried that moving my feminine form could unintentionally harm others, and I never attempted practices such as yoga or breathwork because they could be seen as "New Age" and I feared that by becoming embodied, I might accidentally catapult myself into the dark side. Looking back, I have no doubt that the demonization of my own body contributed to the variety of autoimmune diseases I am struggling to recover from now. It has taken a lot of work to view the vessel of my human body as worthy of nourishment and honor.

Coming to understand a new definition for beauty has helped me find value in pursuing a practice of seeking beauty within myself.

In his book *Divine Beauty: The Invisible Embrace*, the great Celtic visionary, poet, and contemplative mystic John

O'Donohue refers to *beauty* as a call and an invitation: "When we awaken to the call of beauty, we become aware of new ways of being in the world. We were created to be creators. At its deepest heart, creativity is meant to serve and evoke beauty. When this desire and capacity come alive, new wells spring up in parched ground, difficulty becomes invitation and rather than striving against the grain of our nature, we fall into rhythm with its deepest urgency and passion."[3]

O'Donohue's words enliven my spirit toward creating and chasing after beauty as nourishment. And yet I am also exhausted and overwhelmed, and seeking beauty can often feel more like a far-off dream—or even worse, a chore—rather than an opportunity.

I also ponder how, in our current culture that glorifies hustle and short-form communication through text messages and social media apps, we can ever fully engage with tangible beauty if we no longer have the capacity to answer any other calls.

Maybe you, like me, have just felt too exhausted to answer any more "calls" because the number of needs and requests that must be attended to on any given day is already overwhelming. Like on those groggy mornings after nights when I have barely slept, and my kids seem to ask for snacks, juice, and assistance every two minutes. I do my best to respond, but there just doesn't seem to be any margin to put energy into seeking beauty.

I can sometimes even feel apathetic about making pictures. Like, what's the point? Everything is so heavy, how could making space to create photographs of myself make things feel any different? I must remind myself in these times that I may just be tired or processing something that is causing me to need extra rest, because in my soul I am sure that taking notice of beauty is not something extra to write on my to-do list—it is essential for gaining strength to thrive. Noticing beauty helps us to see ourselves and others with tenderness by softening our view of what we focus on. O'Donohue goes on to say that "the experience of beauty is like a homecoming. When we feel and know and touch the beautiful we feel that we are at one with ourselves. Because in some subtle and secret way, beauty meets the needs of the soul."[4] It is the *beautiful* that can bring us back to the peace of true belonging.

Several years back, while road-tripping across the country with my family, we stopped off for a few days to rest at an Airbnb near the redwoods in Northern California. Upon entering the house, we were greeted with a note taped to the kitchen counter that read: "Walk up to the trees in the orchard. Eat the oranges."

This was the only message our hosts had left for us, aside from the Wi-Fi password.

Eat the oranges.

I had never really been one for orange eating. I mean, maybe a clementine here or there that had come in a kid's meal, but I'd never made a point of sitting down just to eat an orange. I was, however, intrigued by the host's very specific instruction. So, on our second afternoon staying at the house, we decided to walk to the orchard. I slung my toddler on my hip and up the hill behind the house we went, until we were waist-high in the tall grass dotted with purple lupines and yellow daisies that surrounded the grove of trees. I set my son down and we both looked up in awe at the branches. The colors were vibrant, and the aroma was citrusy sweet.

"Eat! Eat!" my son insisted, leaping to try and pull down the fruit.

I lifted him up so he could pick a few, and there in the grass beneath the shade of the trees, we ripped open the first orange. The meat burst from the peel, and it tasted like a melting popsicle, so rich and delicious. My boy and I grinned at each other, juice dripping down our chins, and I could have sworn that time stopped, the both of us were so engulfed in delight.

I sent the owners a message after we checked out, thanking them for directing us toward joy. They wrote back, "It's a great pleasure of life! We eat them like an apple . . . peel and all. Juice everywhere!"

There was a childlikeness in their response—they knew they had a portal to beauty in the yard of their Airbnb and were gracious enough to tell us how to find it. I never would have thought to take an orange off the tree, let alone eat one right then and there in the orchard, if they hadn't encouraged it. Their note was a *call* much like John O'Donohue described— not forced upon us but inviting us to be nourished and revived if we were courageous and curious enough to answer.

I listened to an episode of the *justUS* podcast that featured public speaker and embodiment educator Natalie Kuhn. In talking about the experience of joy, she said, "Joy isn't an outcome. Joy isn't something we can get to. It's not a destination. Joy is a frequency that rushes into your life from being devotionally present to your life as it is."[5]

As it is.

We cannot force joy and beauty, but we can welcome them by our willingness to truly look.

In seasons of overwhelm, when hope can feel like a pursuit of little worth, it is often my kids who remind me how to arise from being asleep to my own life. Children seem to be much more tuned in to the hidden hopefulness in beauty than we adults are, as most times we offer a long list of reasons to justify passing it by.

I remember the year that my daughter Mabel turned eight and received a pet fish for her birthday. She had longed for that fish for months and was so happy to receive him as a present. Well, sadly, he graduated to fishy heaven later that same day, which made for quite a sorrowful birthday girl. We did our best to provide him with a proper burial in the garden and a celebration of his short yet meaningful life, complete with singing and prayer. In the weeks that followed, Mabel went out every morning to visit with her fish and make sure that no squirrels dug him up.

Fast-forward to about a month later when she came running into the kitchen telling me I had to come see something amazing in the garden. She pulled me by the hand all the way out there and then knelt us down by the grave, saying, "Mommy, look! He is growing into something new!"

I looked down at the dirt as she cupped her hand around a little seedling in much the same way she had cradled her fish weeks earlier. She looked up at me with glimmering eyes and said, "I wonder what he's going to become? I'm so excited

to find out! What do you think he will be, Mommy?" I had to catch my breath, stunned by the hope that had sprung up within her there at the grave that I thought had been an ending. Mabel was offering me an invitation to imagine and to join her belief in a beautiful future. We spent a few minutes there admiring the little sprout and guessing what he would grow to be. I said broccoli and she said peas.

My favorite part of this story is that later in the day, while sharing with my husband about Mabel's excitement at this new development, he told me his secret: He'd tucked a mammoth sunflower seed there under the soil the evening of her fish's funeral. He looked at me with a glimmer in his eye, not having fully known what an impact that one small seed would have on all of us. I laughed and cried thinking about a fish turning into a gigantic sunflower, and I felt the spirit of aliveness spring up in me for the first time in quite a while. I was reminded that all the joy we are seeking is often born of things not visible from our limited perspective.

It is simply our willingness to slow down and answer the call of beauty that opens us to delight.

Being rigid and closed-minded toward life often leads me to believing the old lies that nothing will ever change and that to soften is weak and meaningless. The harshness of my perspective can be felt and seen in the way I hold and view my body, and it's glaringly reflective when I look back at images I have captured of myself during those times. Our bodies are always sending us messages that our minds cannot yet translate into words.

Sometimes we can feel blocked from creating self-portraits when our bodies don't look the way we'd ideally like them to. In these instances, I try to zoom out a bit and focus on the *purpose* of the photo objectively. If your current state of mind feels harsh and overwhelming, then perhaps a softer perspective is quite literally the mode you could try shifting into. If you

are using a camera that has the option for manual focus instead of autofocus, switch it to manual. Then set up your camera to shoot pictures with an intentionally softened focus, so that whatever you're capturing looks more like a watercolor painting where the hues blend together. Think of these photos as an attempt to translate the landscape and feelings of your inner life into an image.

What if this tangible piece of art—your feelings expressed in photo form—could help you view your life with a little more empathetic tenderness? Looking at myself with curiosity about the weights my body may be carrying is often a prompt I use to enter a space of embodied awareness. I will sometimes sit before a mirror and observe the current posture my body is holding. Instead of shaming myself for being human, I look into my own eyes and offer reassurance that observing myself without turning away is the hardest part. From there, I try to talk to myself the way I might talk to my daughter if she were feeling ashamed. I breathe deeply, attune with my inner child, and do my best to see myself as an artistic work in progress. I ask myself what element or plant in nature curves in a posture that might mirror my own spine. Could I arch my back or relax into a gentler curve?

Photographing oneself is akin to crossing a threshold—we can stay the same, or

> Our bodies are always sending us messages that our minds cannot yet translate into words.

we can make the vulnerable choice to be curious about our own mysterious caverns within.

We stand at the edge of our comfortable lives and try to carefully peer into what transformation could hold for us. It's in contemplating all the things that went "wrong" in the past and focusing on all that *could* happen in the future that we freeze up. We remember the darkness we once hid within, and we wonder if it's any use to keep trying to see ourselves in the light. We want assurance that taking this leap will be worth the costly emotional nakedness it requires. But there's no proving our safety before the free fall into mystery, and that's probably why we get wiser the moment we take the leap.

One of the women I look to when trying to muster the courage to show up for myself is the famous marathon swimmer Diana Nyad. In 2013, at the age of 64, she became the first and only person ever to make the nearly one-hundred-mile swim from Cuba to Florida across deadly shark- and jellyfish-infested waters. The physical feat was, of course, incredibly inspiring, but it was Diana's solid, personal commitment to facing and overcoming the mental and emotional effects of her own childhood trauma that impacted me greatly.

It was about swimming, but on a deeper level it was about *healing*.

In an interview that took place in the weeks following her achievement, Diana was asked what the most difficult and challenging part was about the marathon swim. She said people might think it was the sharks or the blackness of the sea or the strength of the Gulf Stream's current, but it was none of those. She said the scariest part of every attempt was always right before jumping in, while *standing on the beach and staring out at the water*.[6]

To look deeply and dwell upon the foundational elements that have formed our identities can feel like standing on the edge of the ocean. And if you're like me, you probably have

spent a good amount of your energy trying *not* to look at your fears, your body, or your coping mechanisms. Looking at ourselves feels terrifying because it presents us with knowledge that could initiate change. Change is disruptive and uncomfortable and often affects not just ourselves but all of those who live life alongside us. In every picture we take, we have a choice: Either continue believing the same old stories about ourselves or step into the practice of creating new ones. This is the work of breaking generational cycles of self-harm created by the words we repeat to ourselves when no one else is listening.

It is helpful for me to remember that many of the stories I have been telling myself all my life were never even mine to begin with—they were passed down to me by my family, by the church I was raised in, and by a culture centered around personal comfort, perfection, and achievement. I do not have to keep retelling these stories others crafted just to keep me small—and neither do you.

Each photograph of ourselves we bravely choose to create is an entire world of belief captured within an image—what we long for, what we love, and what we desire to embody. We can answer the call of finding beauty in all of our being.

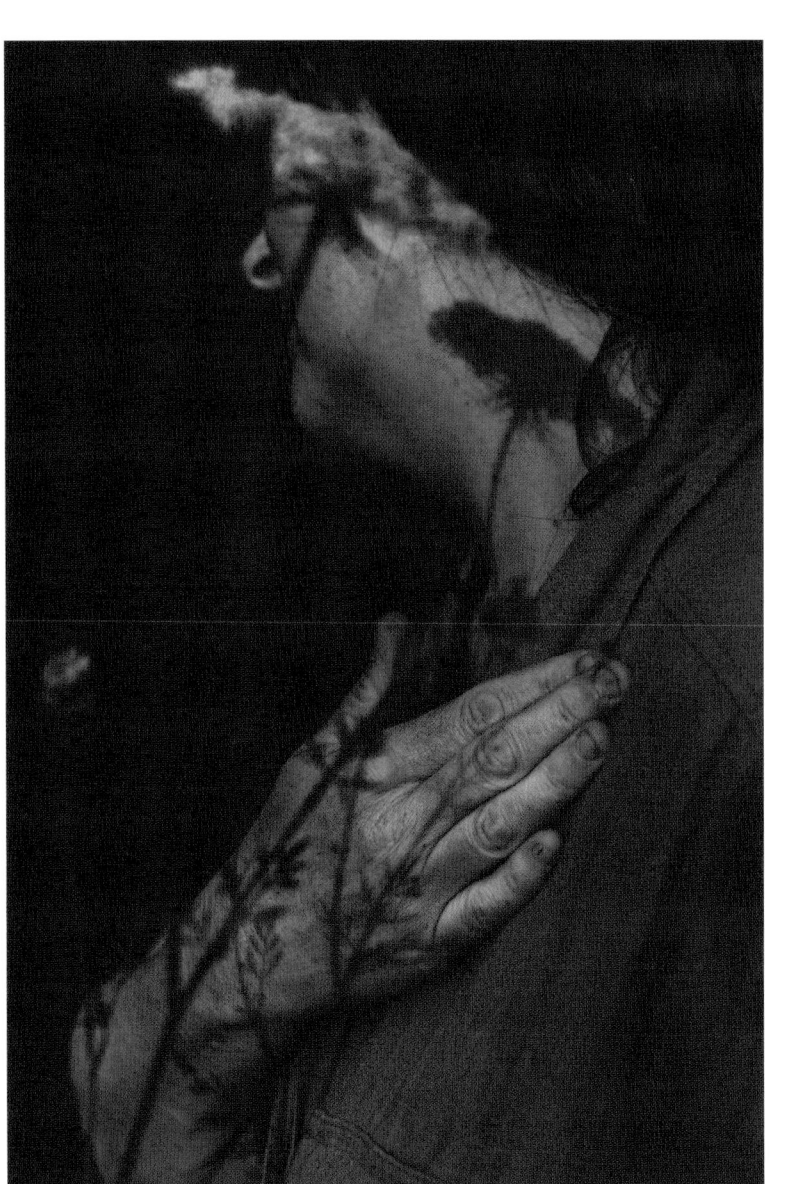

CHAPTER 3

CONTEMPLATION THAT LEADS TO TRANSFORMATION

I don't really know if my paintings are surreal or not, but I do know that they represent the frankest expression of myself.

Frida Kahlo

When it comes to photography, we often use the phrase "*take* a picture." But what if, instead of thinking that something has to be *taken*, we could slow down and contemplate what could be *given* in the process of image making?

Photography, by definition, is the art of painting with light.

As a professional photographer for my entire adult life, you'd think that maybe the thrill of light chasing was behind me. But I still transform into an excited child any time the sun dips low at the horizon and casts radiant beams of gold across a landscape like a blanket of shimmering honey.

Viewing sun flares through my camera lens has, at times, produced in me an indescribable feeling of awe, similar to what astronaut William Anders described when he viewed the earth while orbiting the moon. My entire perspective shifts into a posture of softness and joy in the presence of that blazing light.

In studying about that iconic *Earthrise* image, I learned that what Anders felt up there has been the common takeaway for those who have observed our planet from space. The phenomenon is known as the "overview effect."

Space philosopher and author Frank White coined that term over thirty years ago in his book *The Overview Effect*, which features original interviews with astronauts who experienced intense emotions and transcendence after viewing

our planet from space. Although the intensity of their feelings varied according to the amount of time they had spent on mission, the overall impact was similar: Each astronaut expressed the undeniable interconnectedness of all living things. From a pulled-back perspective, all boundary lines, political stances, and grievances between individuals and nations were invisible. Only a thin green line of atmosphere separated the vibrancy of our fragile home from the terrifying abyss all around.[1]

While I'm pretty sure I will never be one of the lucky few who get to board a spacecraft and experience the overview effect firsthand, the awe shared among those who've had the opportunity is something I long for on a cellular level. Many astronauts, regardless of their personal beliefs, have called their experiences religious or spiritual awakenings. They all seem to agree that *contemplation* shifted their consciousness and their way of being in the world.

Nicole Stott, veteran NASA astronaut, spent 104 days in space, was the tenth woman to perform a space walk, and painted the first watercolor in space (my personal favorite fact about her). She is known as "the Artistic Astronaut" and wrote the book *Back to Earth*. In seeing the fragility of humanity and our interconnected oneness, she felt the urgent need to advocate for the protection of our planet.[2] I have come to understand the art of self-compassion in a similar way. In becoming aware of my own worth as a beautifully flawed human being, I have grown empathy for others.

Contemplation and intentional focus are keys to a shift of personal perspective. When we slow down and choose to contemplate ourselves without judgment, we become open for inner transformation to take place.

I have found myself drawn to the great Christian mystics as guides into having personal practices of contemplative, expansive faith. Mysticism intrigues me because it does not rest on the certainty of any binary belief system but more on embracing the mysteries of God through slow and intentional practices of communicating with God.

Twentieth-century philosopher William James characterized a mystical experience as having four marks: transiency, passivity, noetic quality, and ineffability. *Transiency* means it is something that lasts only a short time. *Passivity* means one receives something from the experience rather than actively giving. *Noetic quality* means it contains a message or content of some kind. And *ineffability* means it is nearly impossible to describe in mere words.[3]

It would seem the overview effect hits all those marks, as do many of my own experiences with photography. I believe that we can develop our own personal practice of compassionate image making to help us embody new perspectives of great awakening. What we think we know about ourselves, about others, and about God expands within the realm of contemplative creativity.

The most impactful and connective occasions in which I have been photographing others have hit all four marks of mysticism. The natural light captured within my portraits never originates from me—it is *given* (passivity). It also typically means something to the subject surrounded by the light (noetic quality). It doesn't last long, as the light is ever-changing (transiency). And often it is nearly impossible to describe in words (ineffability).

In the times I have lifted my lens upward and seen flares of rainbow light appear within my frame, the childlikeness within me erupts, and I run to show my subject the captured image. I watch my own version of the overview effect in the faces of those who see themselves enveloped within an otherworldly kind of radiance. No matter the individual's culture or beliefs, every single time they are stunned with awe.

Honest photographs, if you let them, can become the irrefutable personal evidence you collect, reminding you of your inherent worth and your capacity to hold the full spectrum of our human experience. When you forget what you have been through and all hope seems lost, marveling at the gallery of your expansive journey can be oxygen enlivening the dwindling spark within.

We experience a little microdose of the overview effect when we allow ourselves to find new perspectives of viewing our bodies, our emotions, our "flaws," and our beliefs. By giving ourselves a little bit of space and distance from the intensity of day-to-day living, we learn to see ourselves as worthy of great care.

Iconic photographer Dorothea Lange famously said, "The camera is an instrument that teaches people how to see *without* a camera." And that is basically the point of this entire book summed up

> Honest photographs, if you let them, can become the irrefutable personal evidence you collect, reminding you of your inherent worth and capacity to hold the full spectrum of our human experience.

in one sentence. Looking through a camera gives us a way to pay close attention to things we might not typically be drawn into seeing—photography is a way we give ourselves artistic permission to zoom in and look longer. The camera leads us into being curious, and what comes into view helps us learn to see ourselves, others, and the world as having greater value.

The place we direct our focus is also where we inevitably extend our *power*.

From a neuroscience perspective, practicing contemplative self-portraiture can be healing because the camera acts as our attention flashlight for intentional focus, which provides anxiety relief and sparks curiosity for learning. Also, by dwelling in a moment and savoring it rather than rushing into a distraction, we overcome the brain's negativity bias and rewire the brain to experience pleasure and presence.

I used to think that there was something wrong with me, the way I could just never seem to escape the worrisome thought patterns swirling in my brain. But then in my mid-thirties I began to learn about neuroplasticity and how, from a primal perspective, our brains are *designed* to keep us safe from danger. We are no longer having to escape lions out in the wild, but our brains still think we must be on the defense. This is what often sends our nervous system into a state of dysregulation or causes us to experience the fight-or-flight response, and it plays out something like this: When we are exposed to a negative experience—for example, a harsh statement or something that threatens our sense of belonging (which in primal times might have indicated the need to fight for our life)—the brain instantly imprints that threatening memory so we can know how to avoid experiencing that ever again. Now, the thing that feels unfair about this is that, in comparison, it takes up to *twenty times longer* for a good memory to imprint on the brain when we experience something beautiful and positive. Twenty times the length of exposure!

It's maddening, I know, but it's also somewhat encouraging because we know what we are up against. Learning about that 20 to 1 ratio gave me an equation for understanding the importance of practicing *intention*. The only way to overcome my bent toward worry is to be very intentional about putting myself in the way of beauty for the purpose of balancing the metaphorical scales in my brain toward peace. I also learned the value of slowing way down to notice what worry previously would have had me hustling right by.

The practice of contemplative photography is really a practice of *patience*—we show up ready to create, but we also believe that by slowing down we will learn something in our willingness. Remember, we practice contemplation knowing it leads us to transformation.

Self-reflective imagery requires dwelling in the present moment, longer than the typical selfie that takes just a second. It is the slowing down, the savoring, the just *being* instead of rushing and *doing* that can illuminate hope even when our brain is working against us.

Have you ever taken time to think about the kinds of memories that might have been instantly imprinted on your brain while your personality was still forming? For me, my mom was ultrapositive and always encouraged me to look for the good in things. But I remember my dad modeling quite the opposite—always bringing attention to what was unfair, upsetting, or worthy of harsh critique. I really tried to be positive, but my mind was constantly consumed by the negative. It's like that old parable that says inside every person there is a battle going on between two wolves: one light and one dark. The wolf that wins the battle is the one we feed.

I lived a lot of my life feeding the wolf of darkness within myself, and it felt validating to learn how the brain prioritizes the knowledge of all there is to fear over all that is beautiful and good—we are primally wired for negativity! Gaining that knowledge brought up an urgency in me to be equipped with practical tools for harnessing the light.

> I feed the wolf of light in me by focusing on how to expand my way of seeing.
> I feed the wolf of light in me by validating myself rather than seeking validation from others.
> I feed the wolf of light in me by setting intentions of self-compassion to help my brain.
> I feed the wolf of light in me by slowing down and refusing to rush.

To pick up the camera is a declaration of hope that something is worthy of being remembered and preserved to look back on one day. It is to believe that there will be a *one day*.

Preservation of and focusing on light amid complicated dark times is very, very brave. Within photographs we can embody the feelings that we hope, in time, to embody in *life*. Imagining creative portraits based on metaphor rather than certainty can help us get unstuck from complacency and enter acceptance of self.

The wonderful thing is that by using the power of intention, we can change the thought patterns in the brain. By practicing presence through our acts of creativity, we establish new patterns of thought—ones that can nourish us rather than keep us isolated. Self-portraiture has been one of the most powerful ways I have learned to accept and honor parts of myself that I used to speak about negatively.

At first it might feel selfish to focus on yourself as a daily practice. Hear me loud and clear—there is no need to wait for a "special" day like your birthday to photograph yourself or prioritize seeing yourself with more tenderness. What if you decided that each day was a new opportunity to celebrate being alive in the body you call home?

Most of the images that have impacted me on the deepest level are those I have created to honor my body while feeling the farthest thing from photo-ready. Throughout adulthood I have suffered on and off with chronic hives, and for years I shied away from being documented in photos anytime the rashes were visible on my skin. Intensely emotional and vulnerable experiences have typically been what jump-starts a cycle of hives, as if my nervous system is a volcano and my skin is the landscape being coated in lava.

As someone who has sought metaphor in my daily life for the purpose of sustaining my self-portrait practice, I remember the solidarity I found in nature the first time I witnessed the way madrona trees shed their bark. These gloriously smooth, curvy trees have vibrant red bark, and every year they shed that beautiful skin to reveal a smooth layer underneath. The most interesting thing to me is that even as the trees are shedding, they are also bearing fruit. They simultaneously release the old and create the new.

The madrona trees gave me validation that I didn't have to wait until I had shed all my old skins completely off to begin sharing the fruit of what my growth had taught me. In researching why the madronas shed, I discovered that "one hypothesis is that shedding removes any insects or parasites that may have built up in the bark."[4] They develop a yearly practice of shedding their skin for maintaining health. Maybe that's a good way to think of our own expansion into wisdom.

Ironically, it was when I finally stopped resenting my hives and wishing for them to be gone that they started to get better. In becoming artistically curious instead of feeling upset and judgmental about their presence, something shifted in me. I think that all of us, if we are paying attention in the world, are continually in the process of "shedding skins." We shed the beliefs we have outgrown, the resentments we have held, the toxic stories we refuse to keep telling, and the people we used to be that made decisions more out of fear than from love.

What are the skins you need to consider shedding? Might your body be sending you signs of things you need to attend to? How can you create space to attune to your body and listen to her voice?

One of my favorite books is *Wintering* by Katherine May. In it she says this about the value of the dark season of recalibration that inevitably precedes expansion:

> Plants and animals don't fight the winter; they don't pretend it's not happening and attempt to carry on living the same lives that they lived in the summer. They prepare. They adapt. They perform extraordinary acts of metamorphosis to get them through. Winter is a time of withdrawing from the world, maximizing scant resources, carrying out acts of brutal efficiency and vanishing from sight; but that's where the transformation occurs. Winter is not the death of the life cycle, but its crucible.[5]

Crucible. That word hit home, so I looked up its definition. According to the Britannica Dictionary, a crucible is "a pot in which metals or other substances are heated to a very high temperature or melted."[6] Katherine was saying that winter is the season of life in which everything *melts completely down*.

All metamorphosis requires a complete melting down of something and then restructuring it into a new form. That form is made from the same ingredients as the original and yet is completely new.

I remembered what I had learned about monarch butterflies while studying insect biology with my kids a few years earlier—the butterflies *must* get out of the chrysalis *all by themselves*. If any human attempts to "help" the butterfly out

of its chrysalis, it won't have the strength to fly and its innate navigation system will be altered. Trying to help the butterfly guarantees its early death. The butterfly models for us that nobody can do the work of transformation for us—we must gain our strength ourselves through the struggle toward light.

Metamorphosis is impossible if we are not committed to the concept of expansion. We must willingly *choose* to see the darkness in which we are melting down and changing as the necessary step before claiming our next evolution of freedom for ourselves. It's that forward push of intention to change that provides the ability to soar.

UNFURL

Slow down
and take in one gigantic breath,
hold, and as you exhale,
unclench—
all the tensed-up worries
from your shoulders and your weary back.
Soften your fears about not being enough
and not *having* enough to give.
Let all the versions of you
be present, tenderly held, and *welcomed*.
Go within to the deepest parts—
be curious about your inner structure.
Swim in the warm cavern of your heart's landscape—
the endless ocean of ever-expanding Love.
Feel your own weightlessness while floating free within
 the mystery.

Look for the light.
The light is you.
You are the sun, the stars, a galaxy.
Feel the radiance of your original goodness.
Let the light flow swiftly through your withered veins
the way water moves from streams to rivers to the sea.
Allow the cascading waterfall of compassion to enliven
    your throat,
and let the golden tingling around your shoulder blades
lift your wings *upward*.
You are rising within the dark
and navigating the elements with ease.
Beloved, you don't have to choose between light and dark—
you embody and hold space for it *all*.

PART TWO

LEARNING TO SEE ALL OF LIFE AS AN ART

CHAPTER 4

VALIDATING EMOTION

> In giving voice to what we feel, the darkest cry uttered with honesty can arrive as the holiest of songs.
>
> Mark Nepo

Maybe you, like me, always wanted to be good.

I thought to be good I had to deny the parts of myself that made other people uncomfortable. I didn't know that forced goodness was in direct opposition to true, embodied compassion.

I observed and internalized that there were certain emotions everybody around me seemed to think were safe to feel and discuss—the easily digestible ones that didn't spark questions. And then there were the emotions that were more complex and mostly to be avoided in conversation.

I define the art of self-compassion as a practice of curiously *turning toward* human complexity as a marvel to behold rather than as a problem to be fixed. This goes back to imagining what it could be like to view our own bodies and personal belief systems with the same spirit of exploration astronauts view the endless wonders in space. What would it look like to become compassionately curious about the dark abyss of feelings we were always told to avoid?

I once received a photography session inquiry from a repeat client who posed the following question: "We are curious about a different kind of family photo session. What might it look like for us to make photographs while experiencing the impact of *depression*?"

I spoke with the client shortly after receiving the inquiry—it was from a husband and wife who had a teenage daughter, teenage son, and a toddler. I had photographed their family over a decade earlier when the two older kids were little. The couple communicated that this new session would be unique as the father had recently been diagnosed with PTSD and begun taking medication after struggling with depression for several years. They wanted to create an honest representation of their family in that season with photographs. Everyone in the family expressed willingness to create art that spoke to the dad's depression; it was important to them not to gloss over the difficult feelings. In asking the hard questions, they were shining a bright light on something that, up until that moment, everyone had been tiptoeing around.

This was not the first time I had documented someone who struggled with depression. It was, however, the first time an entire family, including the kids, were on board with the photography experience as a vehicle for creating tangible forms of validating their interior landscapes.

Leading up to our scheduled session date, I contemplated how to make the most of our time together. I wanted to create compassionate spaciousness during the session, free of blame, guilt, and judgment. I wanted to offer tangible ways for each person in the family to comfortably translate their own unique relationship with depression into imagery.

I have found in my work with photography clients that what we are drawn to in nature often mirrors what we are experiencing internally. With that in mind, I asked the mom and the kids if they would try to identify something in nature that could be a metaphor for how they felt about their relationship with their husband/dad and their experience of his depression. They said they would all contemplate this and discuss their answers and get back to me.

After talking with them, I thought about how in the past I had done much the same thing for myself during a season of experiencing my own depression. I had found that going on photo hunts was helpful for expressing artistically what I was not yet able to put into words. I would search out things that had been struck down but that kept growing. Each one I discovered felt like a creative metaphor delivered straight from God. Those resilient plants showed me that my trauma did not mean I was bound for hopelessness. They were proof that I could keep on living—and maybe even thrive—because I had tenderly attended to my mental and emotional wounds.

A few months after making plans for this family's session, I traveled from my little island in the Salish Sea to my hometown in Southern California, where my clients also happened to live. It was the town where I'd grown up, had a paper route as a preteen, and lived the first thirty years of my life. It was where I had gotten married, gone to college, built a business, and birthed my four eldest children.

On the plane there, I looked out the window at the clouds and remembered photographing this family when I was just starting out as a photographer. The photo session was memorable to me because it was out of the ordinary. They had told me how creativity is a part of who they are, so the parents and their kids, ages two and four at the time, covered each other head to toe—clothes and skin and hair—in brightly colored paint. They really made the session into a multisensory, full-body experience. They got messy and let their guard down. I remember seeing the Christmas card I'd designed for them that year posted on my fridge alongside a lot of other families' cards, and theirs stood out for its unapologetic freedom of expression. Although that first portrait session had happened so long ago, it did feel like the session we were about to embark on together had a similar expansiveness of intention. They were entering the artistic unknown with the belief that growth would come out of their willingness to be witnessed. They were not labeling any feelings as good or bad—the entire spectrum of emotion was to be welcomed without judgment or restraint.

On the day of the session, I spent the afternoon driving around town, scoping out various landscapes, trying to decipher what might be the most symbolic place for the creation of their images. I pulled up to a mountainous green space located in the vicinity of my childhood home and got out to walk around and explore. I was walking on a dirt trail near the back of the park, surrounded by hills covered in mustard flowers, when I received a text from my client saying, "My daughter let me know that the metaphor in nature that reminds her most of her relationship with her dad right now is mustard flowers. There are blooms but also there are lots of weeds." She went on to share that her son had decided on clouds "because they are always changing."

I let her know that at the very moment of receiving that text, I happened to be walking through a field of mustard flowers beneath a sky covered in swiftly moving gray clouds. I promptly sent her a picture of me on the hill and asked if it felt like this was a sign we'd found our shooting location for the evening. We agreed that it was meant to be and was assuredly the place.

About an hour before sunset, we met up in that field of gold. There was an obvious acknowledgment of the sacredness of the moment, as all of us tucked phones away and became conscious about eye contact and embodied presence.

Before taking any pictures, we all removed our shoes. It was an intention to embody vulnerability, and perhaps a sign of willingness to receive any kind of miracle that may be available to us. It reminded me of these lines from Elizabeth Barrett Browning:

> Earth's crammed with heaven,
> And every common bush afire with God;
> But only he who sees takes off his shoes.[1]

We all wanted to see.

The session began with the husband and wife sitting back-to-back, leaning into and away from one another. I could feel the energy of longing for connection emanating from them both. I asked them to try to sync their breathing—to slow down and be aware as together they inhaled peace and exhaled emotional release. I stepped back and photographed them as they relaxed into one another just a bit and their breathing came into rhythm. I made sure to breathe loudly right along with them, kind of the way my midwife did for me when navigating a contraction during childbirth.

The couple later told me that those moments of breathing together while being witnessed by the camera were the most intimate they had shared in a year.

Emotionally validating connection is so deeply intimate. Artistic self-expression provides a way to process through and navigate coming out from our caves of isolation and into the larger expanse of what is true. This family made a choice to turn toward the discomfort, toward the heartbreak, toward the abyss of unknowns. They curiously and compassionately turned

toward one another in honesty, breaking down walls of isolation and shame.

For the photos of the daughter and dad, I created a double exposure with the mustard flowers. For the son and dad, I did another double exposure against the changing backdrop of clouds.

I took images of just the mom and dad tucked into the cleft of a giant rock, then documented the whole family together at the end. And when they smiled, it wasn't fake at all—it was so beautifully real. They had tears in their eyes, and their playful spirit was more evident than when we had started two hours earlier. I'm not necessarily saying that anything got healed during our time of making art from their grief, but they made memories of intentional connection within an otherwise foggy season.

The photographs we preserved are proof of their family breaking the generational curse of enduring depression alone.

There was a moment at the end of the session where I looked over at the dad and was moved to tears at his bravery in showing up so vulnerably for his family. I had this surreal flashback to playing at that same park with my father. I had felt so much dissonance and confusion over his depression when I was a little girl. But instead of turning toward me to help me understand, he turned away. As a child, I used the practice of making art to process the pain of my father's depression. Now,

> Artistic self-expression provides a way to process through and navigate coming out from our caves of isolation and into the larger expanse of what is true.

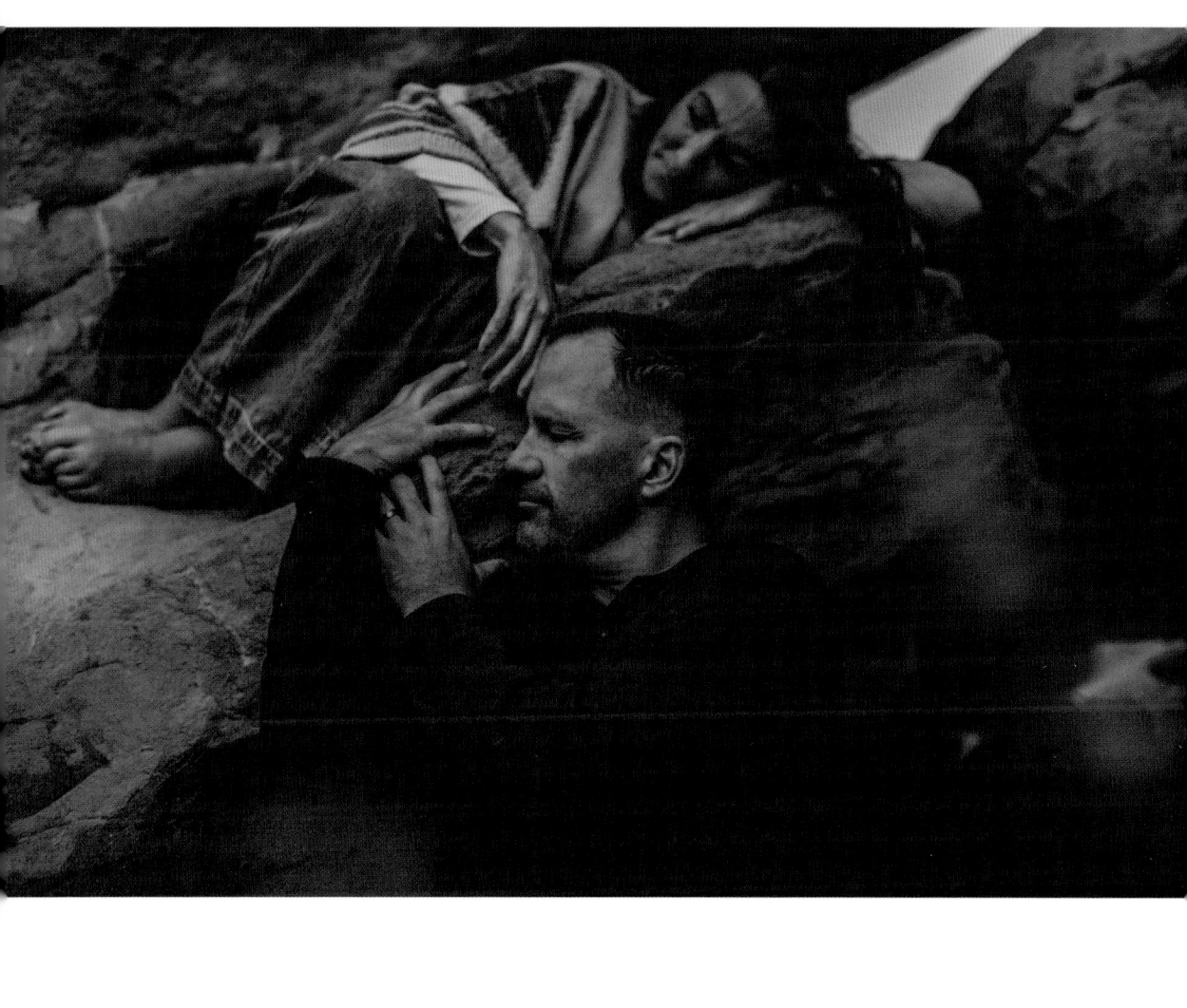

thirty years later, I found myself bearing witness to a father with depression bravely validating the experience of his family's emotions through art.

It was something my own father had never seemed able to do—release shame to embrace his family.

I imagine this couple's decision to make art of their experience with depression was not easy. I am sure it was painful for the wife to bring herself into a space of vulnerability where she could be open to connecting emotionally with her husband after so much distance.

And I am sure it was equally challenging for her husband to release the judgments others may have had about his depression and to be willing to listen to how their teenagers identified their feelings toward him about the experience of his sorrow. He stood before the camera to create emotionally complex art dreamed up by his kids to validate that their perspective is worthy of being seen—and that is some generational-curse-breaking bravery!

After receiving the photographs from our session, my client told me that she showed them to a close friend of hers. The friend's response was, "Can you imagine if this is how we came to church?!"

That hit deep. I knew it meant a lot to my client. She had shared with me the heartbreak of how their church, the one place they had sought support through her husband's depression, had been lacking in empathetic care. I couldn't stop thinking about it for so long—what if we *could* openly and honestly share our multilayered lives, knowing that our questions, depression, and grief would be compassionately validated instead of uncomfortably bypassed?

Our culture seems to have an unspoken binary belief system for emotions that we all have adapted as the norm. There are certain emotions that are unwelcome in social settings, such as sorrow, pride, disappointment, anxiety, and grief. And then there are other expressions of feeling that are celebrated, such as politeness and positivity.

As a child I found that any time I got up the courage to share with someone how I felt about complicated things, specifically in church, I was often told not to dwell on the negative. My curiosity about my own feelings was viewed as dark, risky, a waste of energy and time. My inquiries into complex emotions were almost always met with invalidation of my experience, isolation from relationship, and confusion as to why I couldn't just give it to God so I could be happy already. Everybody in my conservative bubble seemed able to hand off their feelings without any side effects (at least that was what my preteen mind was telling me), so I decided that was what I also had to do to be a faithful believer. Thus began my lifetime of seeking numbing techniques to turn my feelings off. Instead of receiving empathy for what I was feeling, I was left alone. I received the clear messages that mental health and emotional care were a luxury and were only for people who are *weak*. After countless attempts to understand the value of my multifaceted feelings, I decided that I must just be broken and bad.

These experiences of being misunderstood, ignored, and shunned created wounds of emotional invalidation. When our emotions have been invalidated, it is common that we learn to distrust how we feel. Our habit of unconsciously invalidating ourselves can show up in something as simple and as passive as apologizing for taking up too much space, for crying, or for the outward expression of *any* feelings or needs. Oftentimes, invalidating statements we heard as children from our caregivers weren't meant to be harmful but arose because the caregivers themselves were met with discomfort in not knowing how to soothe children's big emotions. The caregivers themselves may have suffered for letting their own unbridled emotions out in childhood and were perhaps seeking to spare us from experiencing similar negative consequences for self-expression.

Examples of invalidating statements spoken by caregivers that over time can become a child's inner critic sound like this:

> "Don't be such a crybaby."
> "You're always overreacting."
> "That's all in your head."
> "Other people have it worse."
> "Stop feeling sorry for yourself—you have so much to be grateful for."

Many of us were required to put others' needs ahead of our own at any cost, to suppress grief, frustration, fear, and sadness in favor of politeness, and to never trust our thoughts or feelings. Such self-invalidation has catastrophic effects that impact our capacity to think critically for ourselves and make decisions that honor our highest good. When our emotional needs are brushed off, ignored, or shamed, we typically do not learn how to be compassionate toward our own pain or the pain of others.

The reality is that very few people have directly observed relationships being repaired in emotionally validating and healthy ways. We are all just winging it with our most precious resource—*compassion*.

I have approached healing my own emotional wounds of invalidation by applying the principles of repair I have gleaned from my research on emotionally healthy parenting strategies. Instead of using the books my parents had consulted while raising me—books that sought to intentionally stunt any strength of personal will—I wanted to be intentionally mindful of the research on how the human brain develops and how validation is the key to healthy emotional growth.

The validation piece is *everything*. Dr. Becky Kennedy, a parenting expert and author of the bestselling book *Good Inside*, says the healthiest way to prevent an experience from becoming a trauma is to always "validate before you understand."[2]

When we are presented with a new idea or when complicated feelings arise, our first instinct is often to *invalidate* by wanting to fix or avoid the feelings. This is what causes alienation in relationships and plants seeds of mistrust. When someone shares something real and we immediately refute their truth in an attempt to "help," assuming that we know better, *it causes a divide*. This is a form of control, not love.

Validation does not mean that the thing you are validating will be forever cemented. Validation is the loving base of healthy and supported expansion. It simply means that you are bearing *witness*. You are making the choice to be present so that whatever growth is occurring, you have a safe place in which to unfurl.

To offer compassion is *validating*, and to offer validation is *compassionate*.

TO CONTEMPLATE

What is the posture you feel your body contract into during times of distress? What does it feel like to soften and expand your body? What allows that release?

SELF-PORTRAIT PROMPT

Create your own double exposure by layering two photos on top of one another to create a symbolic image of your body's curvature mirroring something growing in nature.

1. Photograph something in nature that mirrors a feeling you are currently experiencing. Look for plants bending or reaching to reflect what you are carrying or seeking. Practice looking for broad metaphorical landscapes as well as tiny, detailed symbols.

2. Photograph yourself leaning into the same posture as the natural element you documented. Let your body expand or contract and do not rush the experience.

3. After creating both images, digitally layer the photographs together to create a piece of personally meaningful art. Play with placement and scale to express your internal landscape most authentically. If you are using your phone to create this art, search for an app that creates double exposures and allows you to easily place one image over the other with partial opacity.

4. Make sure you export and save the final image into a folder where you can begin to accrue your own gallery of self-compassion imagery.

DON'T FORGET, YOU ARE A *GROWING* BEING

My beloved plant got too big for her pot and needed room
    to grow.
So I shook her loose from the container (it wasn't easy)
attempted to unbind her roots (it was difficult to do this
    gently)
and untangled the mess of confusion that had been existing
    in her limiting space.
I tucked her into a roomier pot
with healthy soil full of nutrients
and placed her in the sun.

I'll think of her when I start feeling all bound up and stuck
trying to be perfect
and pretty
and productive
and pleasing . . .

Remembering that, just like her,
my only purpose is, instead,
to expand.

CHAPTER 5

EMBODYING AUTHENTICITY

> Lighthouses don't go running all over an island looking for boats to save; they just stand there shining.
>
> Anne Lamott

I used to believe that the most holy thing I could do while waiting for Jesus to return was deny my own worth and rid myself of anything unique, obscure, or curious within. I was convinced that this was my surest bet at being good enough to get into heaven.

I had been taught to suffer well and was quite efficient at it. I first learned to abandon my intuitive feelings in my childhood home, where I perceived my father saddling me with the responsibility of saving him. Self-abandonment was encouraged, celebrated, and even commanded in the teachings of my church. I received the clear and crucial message that my highest calling was to hide away my strong-willed, deeply feeling self. I came to believe that restraining my desires and curiosities was honorable.

Even after detangling from my rigid religion of certainty—you know, the one that comes with a box for depositing any worries so God can deal with the complexities rather than having to process things all the way through—I realized I *still* had to deal with my ingrained aversion to embodying the authenticity of myself.

Before moving to the island, I daydreamed about being able to swim freely in the sea, my spirit calm and my body unrestrained from the opinions or requirements imposed by others.

In anticipation of our relocation, the kids and I watched hours of nature documentaries on the biodiversity of the Salish Sea—and we were completely awed to learn about the bioluminescence that is visible there in the summertime. There was a part of me that couldn't stop thinking, *When I see that sparkle right up close, maybe I too will figure out how to shine within the depth of my own darkness.*

Upon arriving to the island, one of the first things I did after unpacking our boxes was to book a night kayaking adventure tour. When the day finally came, I remember pinching the thin skin on top of my hand to prove that it was, in fact, *real*. That I was awake and that soon I would finally experience the magic. That evening at sundown, I excitedly stumbled out of the van and into the parking lot, flicked on my headlamp, and scanned the almost-darkness for our kayaks. I spotted them on the shore, and as I walked toward the water, I heard my rubbery, ill-fitting adventure gear squeaking with each step—and could not hold back my giggles.

Prior to arriving at the beach for the kayaking tour, each participant was handed an armful of legally required protective attire to wear while on the water. This was the only part I had *not* prepared for.

First was a base layer and our regular clothes, then too-tight plastic rain pants, oversized rain slicker, and a pair of constricting rubber overalls (which made the funny squeaking sounds).

Topping it off were the final pieces waiting beside our kayaks: a life jacket and a rubber spray skirt that looked like the mouth of a giant shark. Our guides said it was all necessary and everyone in the group made sure to follow their precise instructions. No one said a word about the discomfort it all caused. *No one wanted to miss the opportunity to be guided into actual magic.*

I sat down in the front of a two-seater kayak and attempted to put on the life vest, but I could barely reach my arms up and through the straps due to the constricting layers beneath. The harder I tried, the more anxious I became. I did *not* want to wear this life vest. I was *not* okay with feeling restrained.

I looked around at the other people in our group who all seemed to be handling the vests just fine and told myself to suck it up. That I just needed to grin and bear it. I turned to my friend in the kayak next to mine, who appeared unfazed in all this adventure armor, and asked her, "How are you handling this? I can barely move!"

To which she said, "Well, I guess I've just *accepted* it."

I told myself that I could do it too—*accept the constraint if it was a requirement to be taken out to the light.* I closed my eyes, did a little deep breathing and some encouraging self-talk, and finally got the buckle to clasp right against my throat. Then it came time to put on the spray skirt that would lock me into the kayak. *Easier said than done.* When I tried to reach for it, I realized that I couldn't lean an inch without feeling like I was being strangled.

"Help, please?" I half whispered to the kayaking guide nearby.

"I've got you!" he hollered kindly, strolling over with a smile. He spent a few minutes wiggling me into that complicated contraption as I sat silently—the last thing I wanted to be was an imposition.

He secured the last piece of rubber in place and said, "Okay! Now you're safe!"

But his declaration that I was safe very much contradicted my body's feeling that she was not at all safe. The intense panic began with the weight of my furiously beating heart that quickly rose up into my throat beneath the constricting buckle of the life vest. I began to sweat all over as my breathing quickened, my vision blurred, and I attempted to ferociously claw myself out of the layers. I couldn't breathe. I couldn't see. I couldn't feel my hands. I realized that no matter how much I was thrashing and attempting to wrestle out of that horrific feeling, *I was trapped and incapable of freeing myself.* To top it off, my continuous glucose monitor, a device that tracks my levels as a type 1 diabetic, began blaring a high-pitched alarm, adding credible medical concern to my already heightened emotional experience. Two of the tour guides rushed over to help, visibly concerned and panicking a bit themselves at what was happening. After what was surely the longest minute of my life, I was finally able to leap out of that seeming torture device and stumble to shore.

I took a few minutes and walked around, drank some water, and gave myself a shot of insulin to bring down my blood sugar. Once my body was able to regulate and I realized that I was not in actual danger, I became flooded with embarrassment for holding up our entire group from going out on the water.

The voices of shame in my head quickly grew loud:

This is what you always do.
You really are a burden.
Here you are, living your dream, and you can't even keep it together.
Everyone is being kept from this experience because of your drama.

I closed my eyes, continued breathing deeply, and managed to loosen my life vest just enough so it didn't choke me.

Luckily, I had been paired with a professional kayaker in my double-seater, and she kindly whispered to me, "Just relax if you can and I'll do most of the paddling."

She was a high-energy twentysomething who seemed to not have a care in the world, and, as it turned out, she was quite the talker. She chatted on and on without needing much response from me—which, for maybe the first time in my life, I actually truly appreciated. She paddled us along that dark water with the fervor of an Olympian while sharing a plethora of stories about her adorable rescue dog, the awesome van she was currently exploring the country in, and her musician boyfriend. All I could think was, *How lucky she is to be so free.*

I couldn't wallow in melancholy contemplation for long, however, before my thoughts were halted by shrieks of excitement coming from the other kayakers: "Oh my gosh! I see it! I see the sparkles!"

I turned and saw the tiny bits of light exploding like stardust beneath the surface. The abyss of deep blue erupted into pixie dust with every paddle that cut through the water. Giggles filled the dark cove where all our boats gathered as the clouds above us gave way and it started to softly rain. Every drop that fell from the sky hit the sea and exploded like a mini firework, and those sparks were everywhere. It was like being in the Upside Down from *Stranger Things*, except instead of an inverted world of evil, it was a wondrous and magical kingdom of light.

It was mesmerizing, yet I still couldn't shake my anxiety and the suffocating feeling of being restrained. I knew it wasn't just about the life jacket or the kayaking tour. This feeling of being held back had been lingering beneath my skin for a long, long time, and my body was finally letting me know it was time to deal with it.

I realized that the required restraints weren't necessarily bad; rather, the absence of compassion and validation plus the obedience required of me in the past were what felt confusing and harmful. Self-restraint can be a tricky thing to navigate because while a certain amount is important in life, the danger comes when we accept oppression as a way of being. I wondered . . . if I did not have full access to my power, who had I passed my power off *to*? Who had, at different points in my life, benefited from my staying restrained?

In her book *When Religion Hurts You*, Laura Anderson explains how the culture of many conservative churches closely mirrors the dynamics of abusive domestic relationships. She writes,

> Systems built on dynamics of power and control are abusive at their core. Within these systems is a hierarchy, typically built on patriarchy. At the top of this hierarchy is the leader(s) of the group who determines the roles, rules, and consequences and who—in the realm of high-control religions—is believed to be "called by God." This calling implies that followers will demonstrate submission and that the leader's words will not be questioned.[1]

This is a huge part of why handing off our autonomy once seemed like a prerequisite for pretty much *everything*. She continues, "The leader(s) further perpetuates the dynamics of power and control by creating rules for everyday living, relationships, spiritual practices, and how one must think and feel. These rules are underpinned by the idea that since God's mouthpiece dictated them, they should be viewed as spiritually sanctioned and are not to be questioned."[2]

Then Anderson names it—why we trained ourselves to be *good girls*: "Disregarding the rules is often an indication of one's sinfulness, faithlessness, or rebellion. This can lead to accusations of being tricked by the devil, demon possessed, rebellious, unfaithful, prideful, or engaging in idolatry of self, which may lead to punishment, excommunication, or hell."[3]

Reading her book made it crystal clear to me *where* and *when* I had made myself small and invalidated myself. She spelled it out in a way that I couldn't ignore—the reasons I had abandoned myself were many, but all were rooted in abusive manipulation by those in roles of power and a young person's need to stay safe within those terrifying structures.

I realized that my parents had grown up in that same religious culture I had—my father had really tried to assume the role of controlling leader, which was seen as the highest calling for a man, and my mom assumed the submissive, caretaking role. They were both just doing their best, with very limited support or therapeutic tools, to honor what had been laid out in their religious upbringing. I sometimes wonder if what I perceived as an inability to find inner peace was actually my father trying so hard to be what culture told him he had to be rather than embodying the freedom of his authentic self.

In *The Way of Integrity*, Martha Beck writes, "Psychological suffering always comes from internal splits between what your cultured mind believes and what feels deeply true to you."[4] Beck has gleaned this wisdom from decades of work centered around identity and helping people heal. Her writing enlightened me to these two different versions of myself. I had never really given their existence much thought, let alone the gigantic gap between them. There was the me that was programmed to be codependent, disembodied, pleasing, polite, emotionally passive, obedient, self-denying, and afraid of change. And then there was the me dying to be empowered and free.

After a decade of working to untangle the trauma of my childhood, I realized that I had been drowning in that canyon between my two selves, and to find healing I had to figure out a way to close the gap. Something I've also learned since then is that closing this gap is a lifelong process. I will never

completely bring those two versions of myself together in perfect harmony, but I can be continually aware of their existence.

Maybe you, like me, are seeking to unclench from the jaws of a "supposed to" kind of living. To experience wholeness in life, we must release the urge to seek rightness and perfection as indicators of our success as human beings and lean fully into discovering our true selves.

In her iconic book *Big Magic*, bestselling author Elizabeth Gilbert defines creative living as "a life that is driven more strongly by curiosity than by fear."[5] I knew that so many of my decisions in life were based not on curiosity but on trying to stay safe. I always thought I was broken and just hadn't found the "right" fixes yet to be able to function normally in the world. To consider stepping back from my flaws and viewing myself as an unfolding work of art was a wonderfully fresh and hopeful concept.

Francie, one of the locals on the island where I live, is someone who seems to have navigated the threshold of authenticity with a playfully artistic perspective. The first time I saw her walking downtown, I was completely enthralled. Let me set the scene for you: Francie is in her eighties, but if you were to guess her age by her *energy* level, you would think she was twenty. When I met her, she was wearing fluorescent leggings with black skulls, painted high-top Reeboks, an '80s denim jacket covered in pins and patches, and a floppy wool hat. Not one thing matched, but *it all went together like a piece of art*.

I officially met Francie at the pop-up art "unsale" that she held in a downtown gathering space. I saw it advertised in our local island Facebook group and was so excited to attend and finally meet the style maven herself. When I arrived, fluorescent pink and orange streamers billowed from the trees outside the entrance doors like little fairies ushering me in. The whole room was set up with long tables filled with Francie's one-of-a-kind creations, which had the vibe of *Sesame Street* meets Frida Kahlo. There must have been a hundred of them!

The first piece to catch my eye was a rectangular canvas covered in paint and glitter. Sea glass was arranged along the bottom to look like the ocean, and disembodied porcelain doll parts had been pieced together to make up a new figure with a cracked magnifying glass for a head. Wooden spools formed a sort of halo around the figure like a saintly icon. Christmas lights were strung around the edge like a funky neon marquee, and a single, foot-long, vibrant blue feather was glued across the top. Nothing about the art made *sense*, but it did make me *feel*. That it didn't make sense was to me the exact *point*. It mirrored the very lesson my soul was on the journey of learning—that art, like life and faith, is meant to be felt and experienced, not figured out or critiqued.

Each piece of Francie's art was unique and made from every kind of material imaginable. I saw one person embracing a stuffed animal bird with spoons for legs and shells for eyes. Another person gleefully claimed a wool satchel with embroidered flowers and a Star Wars figurine as its button closure. I took my time browsing as the room began to fill with a diverse gathering of island locals. Some were congratulating Francie on her accomplishment. Others, who were just meeting her for the first time, seemed perplexed, maybe a bit awestruck.

> Art, like life and faith, is meant to be felt and experienced, not figured out or critiqued.

I heard someone ask, "What's it all for? Why do you make all of this? And why are you giving it away for free?"

At that, Francie took a deep breath and exhaled, like she was pacing herself before giving the reply. "Well, I just can't stand how people *throw* things away. There is just *so much waste*. And people do it to other people too—just throw relationships away. I can't stand it! So, I pick up the discarded things and make them into something new. Each piece is a character that might make you laugh or think, or maybe it's a world—discover them for yourself and you tell me."

I stood in the middle of that room for quite some time, just absorbing the energy of wonder. People of all ages took *so much* delight in finding their own unique piece of Francie's art to take home and cherish. The only requirement she had for adopting one of her pieces was that you had to "pass it on." And by the exit door Francie had posted some suggestions of what she meant by that: Donate to a charity. Make a meal for someone. Visit a friend. Volunteer in the community.

Before leaving, of course I had to have my own special meeting with Francie. She hugged me, her eyes sparkling as we talked. I told her how much happiness her vibrant wardrobe and energetic walking had brought me since moving to the island.

She laughed and whispered, "You wanna know something, Joy? People used to look at me *so weird* when I first moved here. I was just dressing like myself, like I always had, but it was like they thought my weirdness might infect them or something. But, you know, I just kept on being me every day, and over time, I warmed them up. Nowadays, if I was to walk down the street in a black Patagonia jacket, everyone would think something was really wrong with me! Because they know *this is me*—it's who I *am*."

Francie is the most colorful example of how there's nothing more wildly contagious than authenticity. Just being in her presence made me want to be more and more of me.

In celebrating the most unique parts of ourselves that we may have once attempted to hide, we not only nourish ourselves but also provide proof to those a few steps behind us that the process of personal healing is worth the work it requires.

TO CONTEMPLATE

How might the cultured version of you be different from the authentic version you could *become* if you released trying to keep the peace and retain acceptance? Who were you before anyone told you who you were supposed to be?[6]

SELF-PORTRAIT PROMPT

Go through your childhood photographs and find one that contains the original spark of your true authenticity. Try to replicate that photo of you *now*. It doesn't have to be an exact re-creation but more a reclamation of that childlike light. How were you holding your body in the image? What do you see when you look into your own eyes? Let this be a portrait experience of empowerment.

CROWNED

My new hairs are growing in silver
as if my roots were translating
the voices of my grandmothers,
saying, "My love, well done.
We award you a trophy
for refusing to give up,
for traveling the darkness,
and for singing all the way back
to the light."
I am growing into an old woman
and I love it.
Finally, my hard-won
self-acceptance
is the queenly
wisdom
placed
adoringly
across
my
brow.

CHAPTER 6

MOVING FROM CRITICISM TO CURIOSITY

> We have been taught to fear the very things that have the potential to set us free.
>
> Alok Vaid-Menon

Being diagnosed with type 1 diabetes at the age of thirty-nine was something that forced me to reckon with my habit of using self-criticism as a means for trying to shame myself into betterment.

One morning I sat down across from my son at our breakfast table to review the overnight readings of my continuous glucose monitor, the device that tracks my blood sugar levels and blares an alarm if they are too high, too low, rising too quickly, or falling at a dangerous pace. In one sense, I receive a 24/7 report card of how well I am taking care of myself—which at times can feel bad for a gal who always loved receiving A's on her school report cards. When I am not feeling ultrapositive, it brings up the feeling in me that I am a "bad" diabetic. Every spike on my graph can make me feel like a failure.

Up until that morning, as I sat with my son at our kitchen table, I had never thought about those graphs as an opportunity for making art. In seeing the frustration on my face that day as I reviewed my graphs, my son peered over my shoulder and said, "What if you colored in your graphs, Mama? You know, that spike there looks like a mountain, and where it goes low, it could be a valley!"

I was a bit surprised, I guess, because I had never thought of it. He had, in a mere moment, been able to see with a fresh, less judgmental perspective what I had been anguishing over. In that short but powerful interaction, I began to see my graphs from a completely different perspective—I saw them as a doorway into healthy expression.

I started printing my twenty-four-hour graphs every morning for the purpose of being curious about what I could create out of them, and that practice completely changed the way I felt about my chronic illness and my fluctuations.

When I would have an extreme high or low, instead of judging myself harshly and punishing myself internally, I would try to consider what that spike could become. I began drawing and painting landscapes, animals, ocean currents, and even myself into the graphs. This practice began to shift my mindset from a place of shameful self-awareness into a practice of being compassionate with myself through art.

The colorful landscapes I now make out of my glucose-monitoring graphs are helping to shift my often-harsh perspective toward my chronic illness. Instead of anxiously seeking answers to "fix it," I'm learning to just be compassionately present to what is.

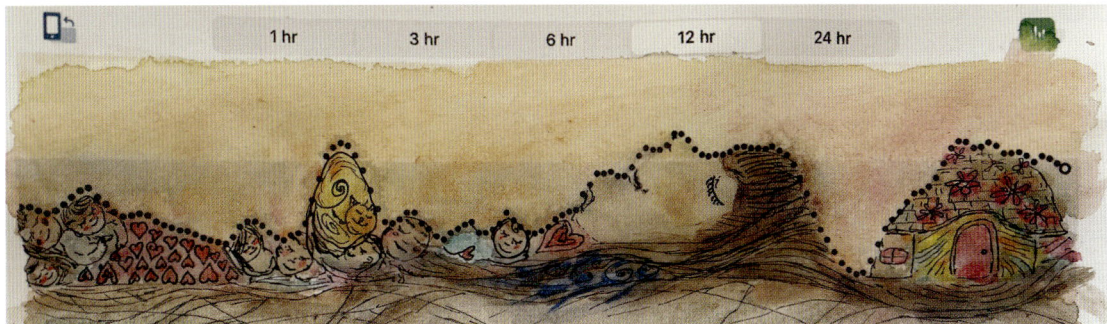
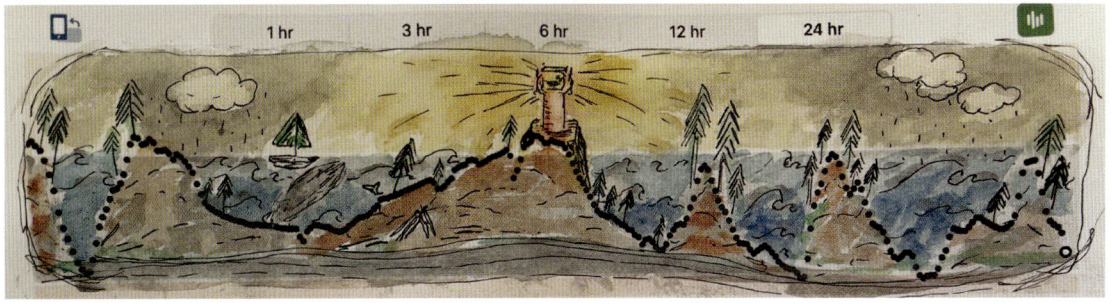

All creativity is born of curiosity—a willingness to wonder what might happen if you *just tried*.

I thought back on times when curiosity had been the portal to expansion. When my bigger kids were younger and we had just started to homeschool, I was trying to figure out different ways to keep them engaged and interested in learning. I discovered how valuable engaging curiosity is for committing to the mental energy required to absorb new information.

I came across the following study that showed how amazing things happen to our brains when we are curious:

> An MRI study by psychologists at the University of California asked 19 volunteers to look at 100 general knowledge questions. The subjects varied wildly, ranging from dinosaurs to The Beatles. The study asked the volunteers to rate how curious they were to find out the answer to each question. The scans revealed that when the participants were at their most curious the parts of their brains that administer gratification and rewards were triggered. . . . The study also found that when we're curious we release a brain chemical called dopamine. Dopamine is the brain's natural wonder drug![1]

This study helped me as a mother trying to get my kids to care about and focus on learning new things. The research showed me that if I wanted my kids to willingly add new information to their already overly distracted brains, I had to find a way to make them curious about it so they could experience the natural release of dopamine. I dedicated myself to seeking out ways to incite curiosity.

This is what we did: We became explorers. We got outside every day and looked for things in the world around us to spark interest. Instead of just staying inside and looking at all the things we always looked at, we set an intention to make new discoveries every time we went out the front door.

We spoke our sparks of curiosity aloud! Research shows that saying things aloud helps the information to be retained and transforms thoughts into multisensory experiences. We asked any and all questions! Especially open-ended questions that enabled us to practice getting into a state of wondering rather than precisely defining. We did lots of unstructured playtime to allow for expression of imagination. Curiosity naturally bubbles up in the absence of being told what to do and how to do it, so we had a very full costume box, fabrics for fort building, and time set aside for daydreaming. I saw what a majorly positive difference it brought to our homeschooling days by helping all of us develop an expansive mindset of discovery.

Art offers all of us a grace-filled canvas to embrace imperfection as our direct route to self-validation and acceptance.

To be an artist is to embody curiosity. Curiosity does not constrict, it expands. It always makes more room for learning. It is not fixed, it is not binary. Once we can be curious, then we tune in and *listen*. Once we are listening to truly *hear*, then we can make the compassionate act of validation. Validating without needing to understand. Validating without trying to make sense of, rationalize, fix, or quantify, but purely to *bear empathetic witness*.

The toxic thought that I must manage my diabetes in the "right" way is rooted in

> Curiosity does not constrict, it expands. It always makes more room for learning.

my desire to do things perfectly—to get that A on the report card of my life.

Marie Forleo writes in her book *Everything Is Figureoutable*, "Perfectionism at its core isn't about high standards. It's about fear. Fear of failure. Fear of looking stupid, fear of making a mistake, fear of being judged, criticized, and ridiculed. It's the fear that one simple fact might be true: You're just not good enough."[2] It was true that beneath my perfectionism was the old toxic belief that I had to be good. For a long time, I thought that being critically aware of my actions would somehow make me a high achiever, but what it really did was keep me stuck and frozen.

Psychologist Flynn Skidmore explains it this way in a video he posted to TikTok:

> There are two versions of self-awareness—there's shameful self-awareness and loving self-awareness. To be stuck is to be in shameful self-awareness. . . . It probably comes from a childhood part of you before you were seven years old. It's the version of you that learned that in order to change you need to be ashamed of yourself, or it learned that if you make mistakes you need to be punished, and the way to earn love and belonging back is to be punished enough.[3]

It was like he explained my whole life right there in a few sentences:

You should feel shame if you change.
You deserve punishment for imperfection.
You are only worthy of love if you suffer.

Skidmore continues:

> What you're doing is using your high capacity for intellect to interpret yourself in the world in a way where you can

punish yourself into oblivion in hopes that if you punish yourself enough, you get love and belonging. The problem with that is that it never ends. What you're going to have to do at some point is choose to end your addiction to feeling bad and choose instead to spend the rest of your life feeling good. To practice loving awareness—where you can be aware of the same things that you're aware of when you're in a state of shame, but instead learn to relate to all of those things lovingly.[4]

A real sense of conviction came over me the first time I heard him explain this crucial shift into loving awareness. I no longer wanted to punish myself into oblivion. I wanted to be emotionally healthy and choose to live from a place of compassion. The mindset shift from shame to love would require me to use my superpower of noticing myself, but instead of listening to the tough-love voice in me, to soften and embrace the parts of me that I once felt ashamed of.

For so long I had tried to hide all the things that I didn't know how to deal with. I wanted to rid myself, my life, and my environment of anything that appeared flawed.

I remember in my early days of motherhood, a friend of mine who was at the beginning stages of building a business around home organization asked if she could come over to get some experience and help me find a way through the chaos in my home. We were in my living room sorting items and she called out to me, "Joy, just look at all these drawers. You can't even *open* them! How do you find anything? You just shove everything in—you're a total *stuffer*."

A stuffer! She called me a *stuffer*!

It really lit a fire in me, lemme tell ya. And my husband (who was listening nearby) thought it was hilarious and completely on the nose, and he has *never* let me live that one down. I didn't like it, but it was *true*—I could see that my tendency was to get rid of the clutter by just tucking it away out of sight to establish some level of mental calm.

Years later, in reflecting on that encounter and my ever-present junk drawers, I asked myself the hard question that I felt ready to receive the answer to: *What did my desire to tuck my mess out of sight say about my self on a deep level?*

I did some journaling and sat in silence and realized that the root of it was the feeling of needing to appear free from imperfection and the inability for me to *let things go*. My stuff was just the outward expression of what I was struggling with on the inside.

I began to list all the things I struggled to let go of: hypervigilance, wasting energy fighting over things that aren't worth the fight, overthinking, ruminating on regrets from the past, worrying about the future, hating my father, thinking I can protect everyone in my life, not putting my health as a priority, unfair resentment at my husband, self-abuse in the form of talking to myself unkindly . . . the list went on and on.

As I was writing out all these things I struggled to let go of, I realized that even though I wished to let go of these things forever, it couldn't be done with just the snap of my fingers. The wise part of me who had been learning all about the practice of self-compassion knew that I couldn't change my brain structure overnight, but that maybe I *could* make peace with those parts of myself by offering them loving acceptance.

Jon Kabat-Zinn, a mindfulness teacher on wisdom and contemplation, writes, "It's not a matter of letting go—you would if you could. Instead of 'Let it go,' we should probably say 'Let it be.'"[5] So, rather than shaming my coping mechanisms and wishing they could be cut off from me, I could draw close to them and try letting them *be* rather than wishing for them to disappear. This felt like a healthy mindset shift. It was a lot less polarizing. It left room for things to be fluid and not judged.

Author and emotional self-help guru Louise Hay was really onto something when she wrote, "You've been criticizing yourself for years and it hasn't worked. Try approving of yourself and see what happens."[6] Approving of myself was a whole new world. There was no metric by which to judge my performance, which felt wonderful but also uncomfortable and destabilizing. It made me really confront how much of my life I had spent seeing where I measured up on an invisible scale of achievement. It all comes down to *just letting it be* rather than trying to figure out how to force ourselves into letting go.

The therapist I have worked with throughout the last few years uses the therapeutic model of Internal Family Systems (IFS), which has given me language and tools for navigating the inclusion of emotional parts I once preferred to be rid of. This model is sometimes referred to as "parts work," and it emphasizes the importance of embracing the full self and living with the eight C's: confidence, calm, compassion, courage, creativity, clarity, curiosity, and connectedness.

The IFS Institute describes this model as "a transformative tool that conceives of every human being as a system of protective and wounded inner parts led by a core Self. We believe the mind is naturally multiple and that is a good thing. Just like members of a family, inner parts are forced from their valuable states into extreme roles within us. Self is in everyone. It can't be damaged. It knows how to heal."[7] This kind of therapy is powerful because it removes shame. It shows us that all the parts of us that arise to defend us within relationships developed to keep us safe within childhood. Our extremely reactive parts got big because we were too little to figure it all out and needed coping mechanisms to function within situations that weren't ideal for healthy growth. This perspective has been crucial in finding peace with—rather than fighting with and shaming—my less-endearing qualities. Thinking of the various parts of me as a wonderfully quirky collection of characters appealed to the artist in me and gave me a new way of holding space for all the versions of myself I had ever been, as well as how they had led me to becoming the diverse person I am today.

I once stood at the shore of the Salish Sea with four of my dearest friends, all of us on similar journeys of trying to heal, forgive ourselves, and move into acceptance of who we are. We'd gathered to bear witness to the vulnerable hopes of one another while also professing, through an intentional ceremony, our desire to release the habit we shared of harshly criticizing ourselves. I still remember the feeling of the cold water lapping at my toes as I looked at each woman holding in her hands an offering symbolic of the desire to fully love herself. Among us, we had vibrant flowers picked from a farm nearby, a poem to be spoken aloud, glittery childlike crowns for each of our heads, and locally harvested honey to drizzle upon the blooms. My friend Ali—or Priestess Alexandria, as we called her that day—recited the glorious poem "i have been a thousand different women" by Emory Hall, whose words are a reminder to acknowledge all the versions of ourselves that we have ever been and embrace each of them as worthy of honor.

Then we stood in silence, breathing in the cleansing, salty air, contemplating the paths each of us had traveled to arrive together in that very spot. We took turns using our fingertips to drip sticky honey onto dahlia flowers and raised them up in honor of the versions of ourselves we no longer wanted to turn away from. We tossed them into the waves with the collective knowing that we could never go back to wishing any part of our histories be deleted. It was a resurrection of hope and a bond of holy sisterhood.

In the years since that experience, I have returned to the shore many times, doing my best to recall that moment of genuine self-acceptance. My friends are scattered across the country, so I don't see them often, but when I step into the

waves and close my eyes, I feel them reminding me to release the shame of who I think I "should" be and embrace all the imperfect parts of me I once wished I could be rid of.

The gift of compassionate validation those women gave me in that little ceremony at the shore was the same gift my son offered at our kitchen table the day he encouraged me to see my diabetic glucose graphs as art—identity as an unfolding gallery of artistic expression that does not need to be critiqued or restrained.

We all can find ways to hold ourselves with more gentleness and approach our challenges with more creativity. Identity is the outward expression of an inward story, and within all of us is a capacity to expand. The art of self-compassion is the creative courage to hold *all* the parts of ourselves with tenderness. The grieving parts, the scared parts, the embarrassed parts, and the parts we once wanted so badly to be different.

Father Richard Rohr writes, "Authentic God experience always expands your seeing and never constricts it. What else would be worthy of God? In God you do not include less and less; you always see and love more and more. The more you transcend your small ego, the more you can include."[8] Love within us is ever-expanding. The more we can accept ourselves as wonderfully diverse, the less we feel the need to do things perfectly or to achieve an impossible standard of goodness.

TO CONTEMPLATE

What do you believe about your own dreams—the ones you had in childhood and the ones you have now? How might the desires and curiosities within those dreams inform the expanding formation of your authentic identity?

SELF-PORTRAIT PROMPT

1. Print out a photo of yourself (or find one that you are okay with using for this project) that is not exactly your favorite from a less-mature stage in life. You don't have to like this photo. In fact, if it makes you feel a bit embarrassed, that's even better.

2. Gather your markers, washi tape, magazines, and scissors to cut out words and pictures to be pasted onto your photo.

3. Time to let your imagination lead the way as you "dream journal" right over the image of yourself. What did you dream of when you were young? Paint that on. Could it be a crown and a wand? A spyglass and a pirate ship? Have fun and set aside grown-up thinking while you create.

4. What do you dream of now? How could you use color, icons, and personal symbolism to declare these intentions?

SEEN

I see you—
trying to be perfect,
trying not to fail,
trying to get it right,
pushing to get it all done
while sacrificing the capacity
to fully *feel*.
Slow down.
Breathe.
As Mary Oliver says, *you do not have to be good*.
Rise from the parched land of victimhood
and stop apologizing for your innate humanity.
Lean into curiosity
and let the fertile landscape of not yet knowing
be the place you finally feel safe enough
to expand
to express
and to dream.

CHAPTER 7

CLAIMING WHOLENESS

I wear myself out and struggle with the sun. And what a sun here! It would be necessary to paint with gold and gemstones.

Claude Monet

C arrie, a client who has also become a dear friend, is one of the gold-edged brave ones who has shown me how to see my life as alchemy.

When I received the call from her, I could sense the seriousness in her voice before she even mentioned a diagnosis. She explained that her doctor had discovered cancer in her breast and that she was trying to make the decision about having a mastectomy. She told me all about it—how she was scared but also felt empowered through the process—and later that day she sent a message: "And I was just thinking about maybe having your documentation in photos be a part of all of this."

Both of us knew what she was expressing—that this experience was *worthy of witness*.

I told her that I was all in, and we made plans for me to travel and be with her a few days after she returned home post-mastectomy if it was decided surgery was necessary. Now, here's what you need to know about Carrie—she is an *alchemist*. An alchemist is someone who transforms an ordinary experience into gold. So, of course Carrie wanted to make art of her mastectomy journey. That's just who she is.

She told me, "Joy, I told Jesus that if we were gonna do this together, I was gonna spend every last drop of this cancer for the good we can make of it."

Her perspective is an embodied answer to a question author and spiritual adviser Liz Milani poses: "What if, like ancient alchemists, we viewed adversity and any challenge as the crucible in which personal transformation occurs? In the historical practice of alchemy, challenges were not viewed as roadblocks but as essential components of the transformative journey."[1]

I've witnessed Carrie's many transformations over the years as her family's photographer.

I had first met her nine years earlier when she and her husband Andrew hired me to do their family's day-in-the-life photo session. I arrived in the wee hours of the morning while it was still dark. In their dimly lit living room, the three of us—Carrie, Andrew, and I—gathered, me with a camera and them with a pregnancy test stick. We sat awaiting the result.

The test was negative.

Carrie cried and Andrew held her until their daughters awoke and needed help out of bed. Then Carrie wiped her tears, lit a candle, and took time alone to journal. Andrew made breakfast. I learned in a very short time frame that this family held authenticity and vulnerability as foundational *values*. They hadn't even known me ten minutes before inviting me to witness whatever emotions were to unfold alongside the result of that test.

They wanted whatever happened to be seen, honored, and documented—not to be looked away from or forgotten. There was a noticeably somber feeling present throughout the morning, but it was an honest one. Tears were shed at different points, but the connection and the joy seemed deeper *because of it*. There was total acceptance of themselves and of one another, including the grief and flaws—they opened fully for it all to be documented.

I admired the rhythms and rituals they'd established in their home—one where mom taking time away for herself in the morning was a respected practice. They had figured out what everyone required for emotional processing and set up a family system of provision. I was so impressed and inspired by the attention Carrie gave to herself—there was a level of self-compassion that felt beautifully validating to me. I greatly respected how no one in her family saw her time set aside for spiritual contemplation as a selfish act.

Carrie and I kept in touch, sending each other poetry and photos of our children. Whenever I was traveling through their state, I would stop in and document their growing family. Once, after a few years had passed and we'd each added another child, I stood with her in the woods when we were both experiencing depression. She had her hands on her heart, I had mine on my camera, and she was telling me how *dark* things felt. She didn't turn away from the truth of her feelings. There was a safety and validation that her honesty provided—an acceptance that all our muddy feelings could be there *and* that it didn't discount how deeply we both loved our children. Her release of self-judgment allowed me to also let go of *mine*.

There was a moment of quiet, standing there among the trees, when she lifted her face upward, and I clicked the shutter. A burst of light flooded into my lens, landing directly above her in the photograph. I shrieked in delight, and we huddled close to look at my camera screen, peering at that tiny little miracle of radiance. Carrie's willingness to be compassionate with herself instead of deflecting or pushing aside her feelings of heaviness set the stage for connection. As of the writing of this book, she still has that photo framed in her living room.

Several years after that, Carrie called me again, this time asking me to document the birth of her final baby. Just before attending their birth, I found out I was pregnant, and somewhere between her contractions I told Carrie my news. She grabbed my hand and squeezed it, and all I could feel was her giving me *permission to feel it all.* The excitement and the fear. She knew them both well. And she validated those feelings in me. In the wee hours of the morning, I was right alongside her and Andrew with my camera once again as she brought that sweet baby into the world. Later that day I came back for a little newborn snuggle and to capture some photos of Carrie's body in all her supple glory. She stood where the sun was casting a bit of light on the hospital wall, her breasts exposed and milk dripping down. I pressed the shutter.

Neither of us knew that photo would be the last one I took of her with breasts.

It had been almost four years since that photo was taken when I arrived to document her post-mastectomy. I let myself in the front door, this time to a bigger house and a much more expanded family than when I'd first met them nine years earlier. Andrew welcomed me in, and I was greeted with hugs from the kids and his parents (who were in town to help). The house smelled of the freshly baked bread a neighbor had dropped off. There was warmth everywhere. It was February and the house was still decorated for Christmas. "We decided to just keep it up, maybe go all year, who knows," Andrew said with a wink as he saw me eyeing the decorations.

He led me down the hallway to Carrie—the queen on her cozy recliner throne—and she smiled big. She was somehow

radiant. Because hugging was not ideal, we grabbed hands and *squeezed*. Ports and drains were attached to her body. I sat beside her, and we discussed several of the things she desired to have captured while I was there. One was the removal of her bandages before she took a shower, which would allow her to *look fully* and see herself without breasts for the first time. We talked about the flower farm she was dreaming of creating. She told me about Joan of Arc and the spirit of saints she had felt alongside her through the surgery. That afternoon I stood with them in their bathroom as together they worked to remove the bandages very slowly and carefully.

The day was full of firsts—a bunch of holy thresholds Carrie was crossing—and by some miracle I got to be there up close as *artistic witness*.

I documented pictures of them standing in front of the mirror, looking together in the light at the bruises and sutures on her skin. The feeling was reminiscent of that very first moment I'd shared with them gathered around the pregnancy test, none of us sure what to expect but knowing it would be *important to remember*.

Andrew helped Carrie into the shower and got the temperature to where it was just right. She stepped back into the stream of water, gripped the shower door, and let out a loud exhale, drenching her head completely in the flow. I stood witness as Andrew *really looked* at his wife. He smiled at her continuously and took so much care in washing the surgical tape residue off her ribs and back. He was fully dressed and completely soaked but didn't seem to even notice. She couldn't lift her arms and asked him, "Wash my hair, babe?" It was obvious that he wasn't sure exactly which shampoo to use, but he did the best he could and the two of them giggled their way through it. I stepped back as he massaged her scalp and just thought, *This. This is love.*

> Maybe love, at its most grand and most simple, is the choice to be present.

Maybe love, at its most grand and most simple, is the choice to be present for whatever life gives while taking great care to be patient and tender with each other's wounds.

It felt like time was standing still. Carrie rested. She ate. She talked about the seeds she wanted to start. Andrew read to her. Their kids did homework with their grandparents, and each one would occasionally pop in for a little visit. Liz Milani writes, "If everything is a portal for our growth and becoming, then that means everything is: the good, the bad, the boring, and everything in between. How can we apply the alchemical perspective to our own challenges?"[2]

That afternoon, Carrie and I sat together and talked about what kind of photographs we might be able to create together to honor, grieve, and welcome the transformation of her new form.

She spent the afternoon journaling words of *life* that she felt needed to be declared right alongside her still-raw incisions. In their house, in an upper room with a window, we prepared space for our image-making. Andrew carried up a cozy chair for her to recline into, and we turned up the heat a bit so she wouldn't be chilly while exposing her bare skin. She made her way to the room slowly and with intention. We sat together, me with my camera and Carrie with her Sharpie marker.

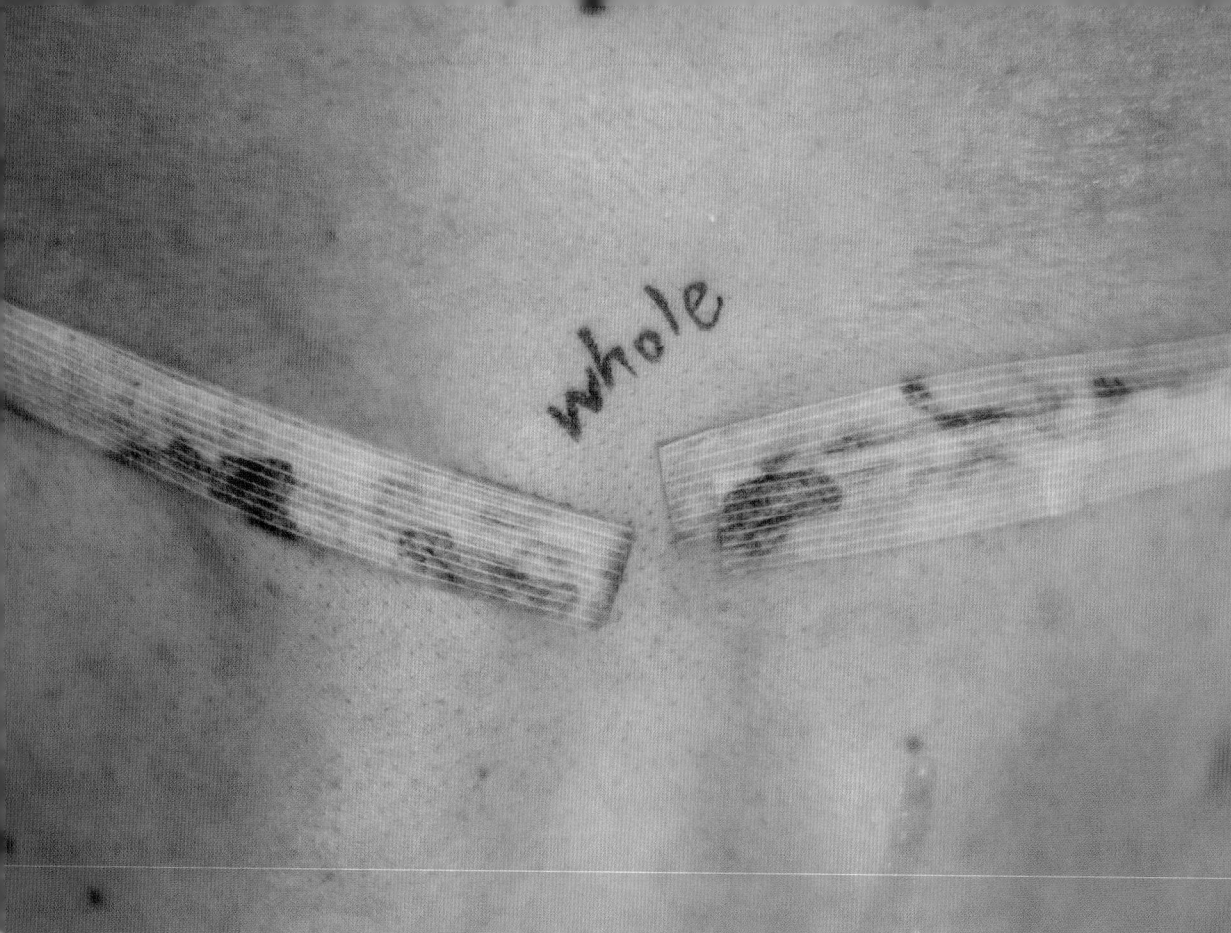

She wrote the word *mother* across her breastbone. She wrote the word *whole* over her heart, in the place where her two incision scars almost met in the middle. She wrote *fruitful* across her belly, understanding that she would indeed mother others in ways not yet known and still unfolding.

She wrote the words *healed* and *abundance*, because those marks left by the surgeon would not get the last word. By the time she was done, her abdomen looked like a poem. I took photograph after photograph to memorialize her bravery so that she would never forget. *Alchemy.*

Maybe alchemy is not one big bid for attention but a regular practice of refusing to give up.

One year after her surgery, Carrie and I were texting back and forth, reflecting on all that had unfolded since we'd last been together. She told me about her year:

> It is because I went into and walked through the diagnosis, the surgery, the recovery, letting my eyes see the scars—it was my choice to walk through all that with eyes wide open—that I am where I am now. And what I mean by that is I know who I am in the marrow of my bones. I think of the cancer—yes, it's a disaster and all that in the natural realm, and also what I knew to be true was that there was endless beauty to encounter in and through it—both for me and others. I am so thankful I had the ability to declare that by having pictures made at the "worst" moment—staring it straight into the eyes.

In an interview with Terry Gross of NPR, the brilliant writer Joan Didion, a brave explorer of her own deep caverns of darkness and loss, shared an idea that I often think back on when contemplating my experiences with Carrie and when struggling to bear witness to my own pain. She said, "I myself have always found that if I examine something, it's less scary. You know, I grew up in the West, and we always had this theory that if you saw—if you kept the snake in your eye line, the snake wasn't going to bite you. And that's kind of the way I feel about confronting pain. I want to know where it is."[3]

Keeping an eye on the scary parts of ourselves seems to be the pathway of alchemy.

In front of my camera lens, Carrie has processed grief without restraint and navigated a spectrum of loss while also offering herself gentleness, validation, and permission to evolve and rise. Time with Carrie has always felt like being drawn into the sacred middle between life that is visible and the invisible spiritual life swirling all around—the liminal space. That word *liminal* originates from the Latin word *limen*, which quite literally translates to "threshold." Over the year, her explorations of the thresholds presented to her made room for me to deepen my once-limited understanding of metamorphosis, love, and faith.

What I didn't tell you at the beginning of sharing Carrie's story was that when I drove up there to photograph her post-mastectomy, I had pretty much decided that God, Jesus, and the whole shebang was something I might need to just let go of. It was just feeling too hard, too exhausting, and too costly to keep untangling the light from the dark.

But then I opened the door to her house and was greeted with the warmth of Christmas lights in February, and I remembered what the presence of true love could be like. I know that Carrie's belief in and dedication to making alchemy of her life is a direct reflection of her belief in Jesus. She embodies the kind of needed and true religion that Richard Rohr describes when writing of the in-between space of liminality:

> I believe that the unique and necessary function of religion is to lead us into . . . liminal time. . . . Religion should lead us into sacred space where deconstruction of the old "normal" can occur. . . . Cheap religion teaches us how to live contentedly in a sick world, just as poor therapy teaches

us how to accommodate ourselves to a sometimes small world based on power, prestige, and possessions. A good therapist and a good minister will always open up larger vistas for you, which are by definition risky, instead of just "rearranging the deck chairs" on a sinking Titanic.[4]

The thickness of love that held me during those two days I spent with Carrie and her family was otherworldly. Her vulnerably raw acceptance of growth and her willingness to let me see it created a holy space of belonging. She showed me that I didn't have to struggle so hard to make sense of my religious confusion and I didn't have to give up on faith completely. Change is the essence of nature. We are not meant to stay the same or to live within the skins of our past selves.

Our spirituality, personal identity, and creativity will be forever intertwined, and as one expands, so will the others. This is healthy, as we want to keep growing and not stagnate.

In a talk given in early 2024, Jason Morriss, lead pastor at Austin New Church, wonderfully provided words to help me understand how our beliefs were never meant to stay the same but to expand as our understanding and empathy for others grows. Morriss said, "We are built to seek, not find. We're awkward finders, we're brilliant seekers. The moment that we think our seeking days are through because we've finally found the object of our desires, everything shifts, it changes, the object moves. And we either move with it or we build a cathedral to whatever it was right before it moved. But listen close—true seekers build tents, not cathedrals."[5]

True seekers build tents. It was okay to not be completely sure and settled about my journey of growth, because the essence of faith is to be open to the unexpected and uncomfortable. Carrie modeled for me that to change could be beautiful, healthy, and necessary. I could find a way to move forward

with a faith perspective that included the acknowledgment of my fears, my doubts, *and* my grief.

Carrie opened a larger vista of belief for me—one where I could see how to be both my full authentic self *and* a follower of Jesus.

TO CONTEMPLATE

You make alchemy of your life with every tiny choice to keep hoping and seeking gold in a land of endless potential for disappointment. Ponder how every photograph you take, even just with your phone, is a way of choosing to focus on and embody hope.

SELF-PORTRAIT PROMPT

1. Sit quietly and ponder which part of your body may need compassion, a place you could focus on with an intentional alchemic perspective.

2. Embrace this part and imagine what *words* may need to be declared there. Then grab a marker, a pen, or paint, and put those words directly on your skin the way Carrie did. Do not restrain yourself or try to make the penmanship perfect.

3. While the words are still fresh on your skin, photograph yourself. (If you have a trusted friend that you feel physically and emotionally safe with, consider inviting them to join you in this practice of alchemy. You could bear witness to each other's courage and photograph one another!)

THE NOURISHMENT OF A THOUSAND CHANCES

By candlelight nothing is a mess.
All the piles disappear
into voids of dark
and there is only gold
luminance contracting.

How can I do this in the day,
I wondered?
Strike a light into chaos
that warms.

Everyone in the house is still asleep,
the cat is purring at my hip,
and I feel the pressure of it
like I'm twenty feet below
the surface of things—

how the day laid out before me
is deliciously and terrifyingly
RIPE WITH BEAUTY—

offering me
the nourishment of
a thousand chances.

CHAPTER 8

RELEASING THE WEIGHT OF SHAME

> Well, I've been 'fraid of changin'
> 'Cause I've built my life around you.
> Stevie Nicks

Maybe you, like me, spent a lot of your life seeking that person who would complete you and become your better half—providing a cinematic kind of love to make you, at last, whole.

I think most of us would agree that in thinking back on all the movies, TV shows, and music we grew up watching and listening to, the concept of ultimately finding our soulmate was sure to bring the happiness and achievement of dreams we all were seeking. That famous line at the end of the movie *Jerry Maguire* depicts it well. Jerry (Tom Cruise), in a tone of passionate conviction and with tears in his eyes, declares to his wife Dorothy (Renee Zellweger), "You complete me." To which she replies, "You had me at hello," and runs into his arms, seemingly to live happily ever after.[1]

I saw it modeled all throughout conservative Christian culture that if I could just find a husband to rescue me from myself, then all my problems would be solved. Well, spoiler alert: I did find a wonderfully kind husband, but my longings for completeness sure didn't disappear. In fact, marriage made me feel even more confused and sorrowful because I was then bound to another human with all his own longings and past traumas, with neither of us knowing how to make the other one better.

For years, I found myself anguishing over what to do when the other half of me could not provide the validation and admiration I thought I deserved. Did it mean that I reverted to being only a portion of myself? Was my worth reduced by half in his emotional absence? It was my partner's escape into his own sorrow just after the birth of our son, Smith, that brought me face-to-face with this quandary.

Smith was just seven days old when an accident occurred. At the time we were living in an old farmhouse on some land in the outskirts of Austin, Texas.

I had passed off the baby to my husband Donny so I could take a much-needed shower by myself. He had swaddled Smith and climbed the spiral staircase to hang out upstairs with our other kids. Just before I got in the shower, I heard him tell the kids he'd be right back, and I peeked my head into the hallway to see him stepping down the top few stairs with Smith in the crook of his arm. And then—he slipped. He was wearing socks, and those narrow wooden stairs became like a slide. His feet flew out from under him, forcing his body backward. His upper half slammed against the steps, his elbow hitting the wood with such force that Smith catapulted from his arms. I saw him in the air and froze. Donny let out a guttural scream as our baby's body hit the ground.

I ran and fell to the floor beside him. I could not utter a word. His tiny, swaddled body lay limp on the floor. My hands were shaking. I carefully scooped him up and brought him to my chest. He didn't make a sound. I felt a gush of fluid between my legs, as I was still bleeding from the birth—my body literally hemorrhaging for my baby. I rocked forward and back and brought him to my breast, trying to wake him, milk dripping on his cheeks. Donny collapsed to his knees, sobbing and gasping for air. He gripped my legs, wailing as I rocked our baby. Finally, Smith began to cry. He cried and he cried. I forced myself to take a breath and made my way to a chair. I sat down, rocking back and forth, back and forth. I got him to nurse a little, but he would only last a second or two between whimpers. I saw a large knot growing on his skull and his pain seemed severe. Everything felt blurry after that.

My mom, who was still visiting after being with us for the birth, instantly took over with our other kids. An ambulance came. I watched them strap Smith's tiny body to an adult-sized stretcher as he cried. I held on to Donny as we both watched it happen, and then I climbed into the rig and buckled into a bench while Donny followed behind us in our car. I gripped Smith's itty-bitty fist as he whimpered in and out of sleep. We arrived at the hospital and spent the rest of the day and night in various exam rooms. We were told that Smith had several skull fractures and bleeding on the brain. He also had bone fractures in his arm. We were to wait on the neurosurgeon and be prepared for the probability of surgery if brain swelling increased.

It was close to midnight. The three of us sat in the dark patient room. Smith had cried himself to sleep and Donny sat beside me weeping. I think both of us were frozen and did not know what to say or do. A woman entered our room saying that we needed to be separated, interviewed, and drug tested per Child Protective Services' protocol for a fall accident. Donny went out into the hallway first and I sat in silence.

I watched Smith's chest rise and fall. I glanced down at my clothes. My pants were stained with blood and my shirt was soaked through with milk. I was told not to nurse him so there wouldn't be anything in his stomach if he needed to be rushed into brain surgery. I wanted to pray, but I just could not think of the words. After a while, Donny returned, and then I went to be interviewed. I watched the woman watching me.

"Has your husband ever done anything to harm your children?" she asked.

I could barely speak. "No. Never!"

"Did he drop your son down the stairs on purpose?"

I wanted to scream. "No! No! It was an accident!" I hadn't blamed him for one second. I knew that it could have just as easily happened to *me*.

She finished the investigation for the night, saying everything seemed okay but she would need to follow up with a home visit once we were released to check on the well-being of our other children. I understood, but still, it was almost unbearable. After CPS left, some nurses came to transfer us to the pediatric ICU. I remember them being very kind, swaddling Smith and placing him into a medical bassinet in the room. Donny knelt above him, his arms wrapped around the glass.

I curled onto the plastic couch in the corner of the room, pulled my knees up to my chest, closed my eyes, and slept until the sun came up. The neurosurgeon came in first thing in the morning. We braced for the worst. He looked at his chart, began telling us various confusing medical things, then looked up at us both and said, "You are incredibly lucky. It looks like the skull fractures should heal on their own and the blood pooling around the brain should absorb right back in. We will plan to see you for a follow-up in our office in a

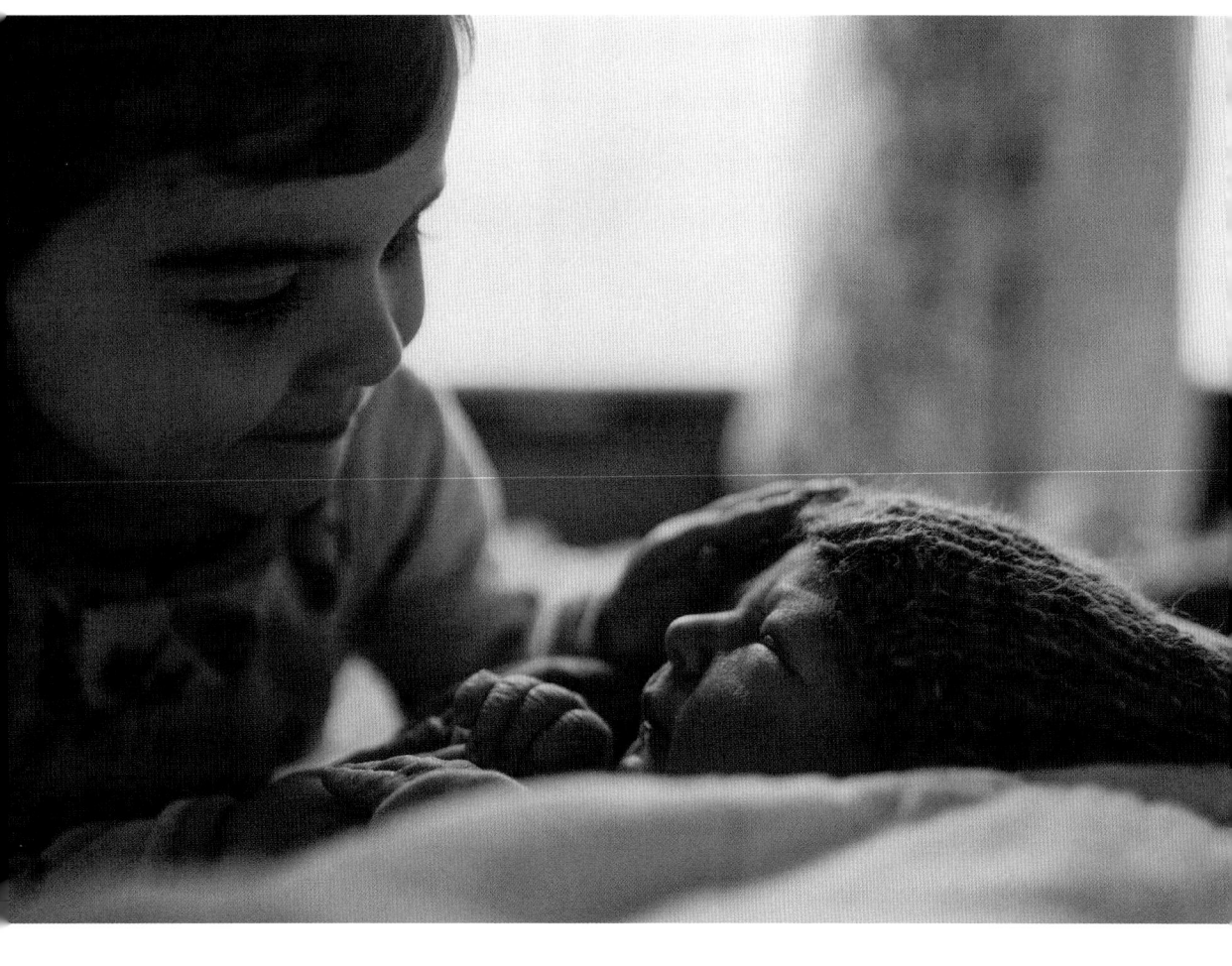

few weeks!" He told me I could nurse my baby. We were in complete disbelief—a mix of intense gratitude and shock.

We went home, exhausted and in awe at what had just occurred. We attempted to resume life as usual. Smith still had a large knot on his head from the fractures and bleeding, and his arm was bound to his torso with a bandage to keep steady the bone breaks they had found. We had the CPS home visit and were cleared of any wrongdoing. In the weeks that followed, I tried to rest as my body was still recovering from the birth. Donny would swing from overwhelming happiness that our son was alive to complete despair about the fact that he had been the one holding him when it all happened.

Over the next few months, I saw him retreat into sorrow, and he became very hesitant to hold Smith. He carried so much blame for the accident, and he began to speak to me about it less and less. He no longer wanted to go near the stairs. Outside of our closest loved ones, he didn't talk to anyone about the fall. He spent a lot of time gazing at Smith in my arms, anguished and destroyed. The more I tried to talk to him about it, the more he pulled away. Anytime the children would go up or down the stairs, he would be triggered. And for me, anytime Donny's voice rose above normal, my entire body would jolt, remembering his scream the moment the fall happened.

Fear took up residence inside of me while shame entangled my husband. It became the norm that we slept facing away from each other. I would reach for him, but he would often just curl away into himself. I felt so alone. I longed to be held again.

I wish I could say that this was a season that brought us closer together, but it didn't. What it did was teach me how enmeshed I was with my husband's emotions. His sadness took me down like a sinking ship because I had never learned how to be grounded within myself. There was a lot of sadness, but also resentment and anger. I couldn't understand why he was pulling away.

I wrote this poem during that time, and in reading it now, I see how much of my self-worth I had placed in Donny's capacity to provide for me:

> My cheeks turn into clouds
> made of freckles in the summer.
> If my partner never sees them
> because he no longer looks at me,
> are they still beautiful?

I had relied on him throughout our entire marriage to validate my value and worth as a person, so when he did not have the capacity to give me that in his grief, I became painfully aware I had to find a way to find love from within.

When he was not able to hold me, I had to learn how to hold myself.

We moved out of that house before Smith was even a year old. The staircase had become just too triggering to climb. All Donny could see was the accident. Smith had recovered perfectly, but a wall of guilt remained. In the years that followed, both of us committed to personal and marital therapy. Donny worked on trying to forgive himself, and I dove deep into learning practices of self-compassion. That time of learning about ourselves was the springboard into moving from a relationship of unhealthy enmeshment to the pursuit of personal groundedness.

Over time, I was able to have a more objective understanding of the unfair requirements I had subconsciously placed upon him for keeping me emotionally stable. My therapist helped me create tools I could turn to when I found myself triggered by wounds of abandonment. I went for a lot of walks in nature. I learned specific forms of breathwork to bring me back into my body when I found myself spinning out inside my mind. So much growth happened for both Donny and me in that season, but in a sense, we also were living in isolation—from one another and from community.

When Smith was two years old, I was contacted by a woman named Tiffany Scott. She was interested in hiring us to make a cinematic-style film to tell the backstory of her family's nonprofit organization.

Their organization was created to honor the memory of their son Truman, who had died at the tender age of three from a tragic self-inflicted accident on the family's front porch. Listening to the details of his death and all their family had gone through in the years that followed was heartbreaking, and both Donny and I felt an immediate connection to them and their mission.

We began collaborating on the project a few months later and grew incredibly close with Tiffany and Tim, Truman's parents, because of the sensitive nature of the work. The cinematic film we were helping them produce not only told the story of loss but also depicted the healing impact that community support could have for families experiencing grief. They felt it was crucial to convey the message that no one can heal from the grip of grief or guilt in isolation.

We were with the Scott family filming along a river in the Ozarks, and we planned to record some clips at the river's edge on our last evening. The scene would be a symbolic re-enactment of Tim's baptism, which he told us had occurred the evening after Truman's funeral. The Scotts were sure they wanted this part of their story included in the film so others could witness the mysterious presence of hope right alongside the guilt Tim had carried in feeling responsible for the death of his son.

This was our second day of filming, and up to that point most of the footage had been centered around the anguish of their loss. Many times as Tim was openly grieving, I would see Donny experiencing his own depth of emotional resonance, but I tried to keep from asking too many questions about how he was feeling. I felt a quiet hopefulness of anticipation rising within me but didn't want to assume anything would come of it. I was, however, praying constantly for a connection of some kind to happen that would ease Donny's internal suffering even slightly from being in the presence of the Scott family's vulnerably tender compassion.

The filming location for the baptism scene happened to be in a spot where two rivers converged—one cold and the other warm. The Scotts had chosen that specific place because of the symbolism it held for Tim and Tiffany in their own independent journeys of healing. The cold and warm streams were opposites, each going at their own pace but coming together to form a collective strength.

As we walked through the looming darkness toward the water, fireflies appeared everywhere, which made all the kids in their family giddy as they ran around trying to catch them. It felt like all the outward sorrow expressed in the filming up to that point had carved out space for something

else—*joy*. We had been so focused on the seriousness of the day, and the fireflies felt like a holy encouragement to play. As we all ran around chasing the tiny bursts of light, we noticed a fog starting to roll in over the water. I hollered out to Tiffany that we may want to start filming before it got too thick, and we all headed to the riverbank.

The moon began to rise over the flowing water before us, and we stood frozen there in complete awe. It was a huge, full orange moon. Orange—the color of the T-shirts the Scott family had made for their organization and were all wearing that day, as it was Truman's favorite color. That moon was a gift of confirmation to us all that we were exactly where we were meant to be. As the minutes passed, the vibrancy of the orange only intensified, casting a bright golden glow on the fog beneath it. I mean, it looked like a million-dollar film set—surreal and heavenlike.

As we all watched the beauty unfold before us, we were vibrating with excitement. Tiffany and I moved into position for the best filming view of Tim as he stepped forward into the rushing waves. I kept looking around, trying to find Donny, but I also didn't want to miss this incredible moment and had to keep my hands on the camera. As Tim began to walk out into glorious light, it evoked an otherworldly level of awe within all of us standing on the shore as witnesses.

Tim dunked himself down and rose up like a little boy on Christmas morning, splashing in the radiance with delight. As I continued filming, out of the corner of my eye I saw Donny run toward the river and then dunk himself down into the water next to Tim.

In the minutes that followed, the two of them played like goofy little boys, laughing, hollering, and carrying on. Tiffany was right next to me, poking me with her elbow and saying, "Joy! Are you seeing this? Are you *seeing* this?!" Gosh, was I seeing it! I saw my husband experiencing a freedom that had been absent for two years. I couldn't keep filming because of the tears running down my face. And inside I felt both shock and overwhelming gratitude. Donny didn't tell me what caused him to run into that water, but I am sure glad he didn't hesitate to go right in.

The next day it was like Tim and Donny were best buddies who had known each other all their lives. They borrowed each other's clothes and made jokes about weird stuff that made no sense to me and Tiffany—truly it was the embodied sweetness of an innocent childhood friendship. I witnessed a genuine transformation in my husband that I still cannot explain.

Through the vulnerable expression of his own grief over the days leading up to that moment, Tim modeled for Donny how not to hide from darkness—how to feel the hard feelings and

express them all the way through without restraint. Their family modeled that *grief can live alongside joy*. Because of that, my husband no longer believed he needed to torture himself as penance for falling.

Tiffany and Tim's fierce advocacy inspires me deeply. They have made it their life's mission to share with the world the message that every moment matters. On our fridge I keep a sticker from their organization in the shape of Truman's tiny hand that says *Moments Matter*.

The Scotts modeled for Donny and me that you can't wait for life to be perfect before you decide to love and forgive yourself. It must be a conscious choice made day after day after day.

Perhaps even more important, they showed us that healing cannot happen in isolation. Attempting to find healing on your own is like trapping yourself inside a fun house full of mirrors: No matter which way you turn, you never find clarity, only warped views that reflect back confirmation of all the untrue stories spoken by your shame-filled self. Compassionate community support is not a rescue boat of saviorism—it is steady ground to rest upon while you gain your strength to escape the all-encompassing depths.

It has been eight years since the accident with our son Smith. He is a vibrant, healthy boy with a fiery personality who keeps both Donny and me continually on

> You can't wait for life to be perfect before you decide to love and forgive yourself. It must be a conscious choice made day after day after day.

our toes. We have all grown a lot since the experience of the fall. Whereas I once believed that I needed my husband to complete me, I now understand that my loneliness in relationship was a longing for connection with the image of God I bear deep within *myself*. I wasted so much energy throughout so many years seeking validation from *outside* of me to feel stable, when the groundedness I needed to feel peace was available right beneath my own feet.

Whenever I find myself holding resentment toward my husband during times of stress, I think about those two converging rivers in the Ozarks—one warm, one cold. I remind myself that it's okay for us to process things at different speeds and in different ways because I don't need him to be anything other than authentically himself. It's what I know he wants for me too.

In learning to be compassionate with my own flaws, I have also learned how to be compassionate with his. Once I let go of needing him to complete me, I had a lot more space to appreciate who life has led us *both* to become.

TO CONTEMPLATE

What are the experiences in which you sense yourself isolating from others? What untrue beliefs about yourself repeat in your mind when you pull away from others? How could creating an intentional photograph with a trusted friend help to defuse those untrue, ever-circling shame stories?

SELF-PORTRAIT PROMPT

How might you create an image of yourself basking in the light of belonging? We can see our own value reflected back to us within the authentic presence of a true friend.

Create a photograph of depth with a friend—a special portrait just for the two of you! Or have a friend create an image of you while expressing yourself without restraint. Try not to think about the camera or the quality of the photo. Just let your body and face reflect the feeling of being seen, known, and appreciated by your person. Let it be deeper than a selfie . . . take your time and allow yourself to absorb the nourishment of playfully creative companionship.

RELEASE

I felt the weight of the world on my shoulders.
Arms aching and back weary,
I tried to walk, hunched over,
when I heard her whisper—
"I can take it. Kneel down and touch your palms
    into my soil."
I was too tired to argue,
so I did it.
Pressed myself down into the mossy Earth
and felt her receive my pain.
The frequency of love rushed through
my muscles
my cells
my hesitation
my fears—
She received them all
without limit.
Love is always waiting, it seems,
for us to lay it all down
rest and receive.

CHAPTER 9

EMBRACING JOY

> Sometimes your joy is the source of your smile, but sometimes your smile can be the source of your joy.
>
> Thich Nhat Hanh

For twenty years, I never showed my teeth when people would tell me to smile for a picture. I would just give a little grin with my lips, always making sure that my imperfect teeth were hidden.

I had been grinding my teeth and clenching my jaw all my life. My neck and face ached at times because of it, and I had avoided dental appointments in adulthood—I was way too scared to know what it really looked like in there. I knew that my mouth told the story of my shame, my fears, and the coping mechanisms I tried to never let show. And so—I just stopped smiling. The shame was even more intense because I felt like this was a fault I had inherited from my father. The last time I had seen him, all his teeth had fallen out. He'd stopped caring for his physical self before I was even born, and I never remembered him smiling without restraint.

Starting in my early thirties, I began doing inner child work in an effort to address the root cause of chronic migraines and shoulder, neck, and jaw pain. Over the next ten years I tried so many things in seeking relief—talk therapy, somatic stress release, energy healing work, healing prayer, tapping, sound frequency therapy, acupuncture. But while the therapies helped to release a lot of trapped emotions and stress, the pain remained. I had somehow adapted to living with it by taking lots of pain meds and grinning without showing my teeth.

I thought I was doing a good job of hiding it all, until my client and friend Laura, who lived in Ohio, mentioned something to me about it. I had been her family photographer for years and knew she was a dentist, but it wasn't something she and I usually discussed. We talked more about motherhood and the creative process of taking pictures and writing. So I wasn't sure how to react when Laura texted me one day in the midst of our regular ramblings: "Joy . . . I just want you first to know that I think you are so beautiful. I see you. And when you are ready, I would love to give the gift of the art I make with my hands. The gift of helping to restore your smile!"

I wasn't sure how to take that when I first read it. Of course it was the most unbelievably generous offer. I also felt completely exposed. She had noticed. She had seen me hiding. I thanked her in the best way I knew how over a text message, and then somehow I let years go by. I don't think I was ready to address the issue of my teeth yet. I knew there was a lot of shame there and I didn't yet have the courage to look.

Fast-forward to 2023. My family was preparing to move to the West Coast from where we had been living in Tennessee, which would put a much greater distance between me and Laura. Though it had been so long since she had offered the gift, I felt the nudge to contact her. *What if she was no longer able to give it? Or didn't have time?* I didn't want to be a burden; I didn't want her to feel obligated. Basically, I could think of a hundred reasons not to ask. To avoid. To keep hiding. I thought about my father's teeth and how he never kept any appointments for his health. In a moment of conviction and trying to honor Little Joy, I sent the text. I knew the lack of knowing would haunt me if I didn't at least try.

"Hi Laura! I would love to talk to you about something you talked to me about years ago . . . about my teeth. I'm not sure if you even remember. Stress has kept me grinding them my whole life and I'm so embarrassed about it. I feel so sheepish bringing this up now. Please forgive me if this is a completely wild thought."

Within minutes, Laura replied saying she would be honored to help, would love to be my dentist, and that she thought I was brave for contacting her about it. We sent messages back and forth and made plans for me to drive up the following week for the first of several appointments. I was so excited and deeply touched by her compassion, and also—I was scared. I texted her the day before my scheduled visit: "I'm sure you work with a lot of people that spill out their stories as so much vulnerability is connected to people's teeth, but I am hoping I don't just become a blubbery mess the moment I see you because this just means so much."

What she wrote back broke my heart and exploded it with love:

> It is vulnerable, and our teeth seem to hold so many stories: a young, exhausted mother's chipped tooth from a toddler bumping; a missing tooth removed during wartime service; a boy who wants to keep his gap in his smile because it's just like his grandfather's. And we also listen to stories of abuse survivors. There are addiction overcomers ready to restore the broken damage. Adults bullied as kids for crooked teeth now wondering if it's too late or if they really care anymore. Usually if they are honest enough, they do still care, but need to find

Embracing Joy • 165

a place to do it for themselves and loved ones and not just because they were made fun of for it. It really is an incredibly humbling profession I've had the joy and experience to hold.

Laura's level of comprehension and lack of judgment for human experience was stunning. I had never heard someone talk about dentistry with such passion for the stories beneath its need. It was clear that her work was her art. It was also her ministry. I crawled into bed that night reading and rereading her words. I felt like I was being given divine permission to begin looking at the layers of my self-harm that needed to be processed.

My alarm woke me up while it was still dark, and I got in the car to drive north. When I arrived at the dentistry office at 10:30 a.m., Dr. Laura kindly welcomed me and got me set up with one of the women on her team. I came to think of them not as hygienists but as teeth doulas because the supportive feminine energy flowing through that building reminded me of a holistic midwifery group. I already felt held and loved. They took a series of photos with microscopic cameras—the technology blew me away. Then Dr. Laura pulled a giant screen around to show me a complete 3D rendering of my mouth compiled from over a hundred photographic images.

"Are you ready to look and see, Joy?" she asked, grinning at me.

I was shaking like it was freezing even though I was warm. She gripped my hand. I took a deep breath and exhaled. "I'm ready."

She turned the screen toward me. It was like something out of the future. If the Avengers had a dentist, they'd have pulled up a hologram like this. I couldn't believe what I was seeing. I was viewing myself from a normally impossible perspective. It was too much to take in at once. My teeth were projected as a huge image and I could see every bit of texture right up close. I saw the damage. I saw how my mouth had held all of the frustration, anguish, and sorrow I never knew what to do with. Sitting in that dental chair, I realized that the pain I'd endured for over a decade had in fact come from my subconscious clenching—an inability to soften and release. I had somehow blocked myself from seeing that I was self-mutilating with my teeth.

Dr. Laura pointed to the image. "Look here at the enamel—that is the *armor* that protects the rootedness of your teeth. Your armor is nearly worn away—you can see here how it has taken the impact of your battles."

She held my hand as I grieved and handed me a tissue when I couldn't stop crying. The longer I allowed myself to look at the parts of me I had hidden—with her beside me, not judging but only loving—the less ashamed I felt. We talked about a plan to go forward and what I could expect. I would be coming back to have crowns put on my front teeth and for the work to be completed. Then Dr. Laura fitted me for a night guard to help with grinding and explained how by wearing the guard on my teeth, it would rewire the neural pathways in my brain to seek a different route for stress release. Just . . . wow! For so long I had been engaging in talk therapy in my attempts to do the very thing she now said was possible—rewire my brain to embody healthier ways of coping. She had first witnessed me hiding my smile all those years earlier and now was personally tending to my full-body healing. She knew that dentistry wasn't about having perfect teeth; it was about being healthy and free to not restrain smiling.

Ten days later I drove back up to Ohio for my final appointment. With gentle, steady, grace-filled hands, Dr. Laura installed brand-new, shiny crowns over my six upper front teeth. As she worked, she told me that in dentistry, treatments like crowns are called restorations.

"Joy, you and I know it now. How the restoration goes beyond the physical, past the transformation of the tangible. You now have a *new* kind of armor—resiliently more beautiful than ever."

To hear an artist, so clearly a master at her craft, speak so profoundly about *teeth* left me awestruck. She handed me a mirror to look at myself when they were complete, and I prepared myself for seeing the resurrected me. I hesitantly pulled my lips back to reveal the teeth beneath and then—I smiled. A big one. Really big so that I could admire the beautiful upward shape of my mouth. I felt a big stretch, knowing that here were muscles I hadn't fully expanded in a long time. I never in my life could remember claiming happiness for myself. I think I had somehow convinced myself that happiness was not real. And if it did happen to be real, it must just not be for me. But when I looked at myself in the mirror after the smile restoration was complete, I realized that God wanted me to be happy.

I felt like all my shame had been replaced with joy. I never thought it could happen, but Dr. Laura believed. She saw my smile long before I could.

She saw me as Joy when I still did not believe it was a name I could embody.

People often talk about being "called" to a certain work, and I thought I understood that. But seeing Dr. Laura in her dentistry office, I knew this was what Frederick Buechner must have meant when he said, "The place God calls you to is the place where your deep gladness and the world's deep hunger meet."[1]

I think maybe any work, practice, or relationship we enter into with a posture of compassion and a mindset of curiosity is apt to become an intersection where our deep gladness can provide the nourishment others so desperately need. That evening after my final appointment, as I was driving home from Ohio to Tennessee, I texted Dr. Laura a voice message expressing all my gratitude. My mouth was still a bit sore, but I had to pour out my heart while the revelations were fresh. I thanked her for seeing my shame and reaching out with compassion when no one else did. She simply texted me back a link to a 2022 news article from *The Guardian* and then the following words:

"Joy—I see you. Read this and know that I'll keep noticing."

I pulled off the highway to stop for gas and to read and absorb the article, which was about US swimmer Anita Alvarez, who lost consciousness during her event at the World Aquatics Championships

> "The place God calls you to is the place where your deep gladness and the world's deep hunger meet."
>
> —Frederick Buechner

and sank to the bottom of the pool. According to the article, "The US team coach, Andrea Fuentes, quickly noticed that something was wrong and dived fully clothed into the water to pull Alvarez to the surface. Alvarez, who was not breathing when she was dragged to the side of the water, was then taken to the pool's medical centre." Fuentes was quoted as saying, "She is a competitor who pushes herself to the limit, and sometimes beyond it. . . . I was scared because I saw she was not breathing, but now she is doing very well. She only had water in her lungs, once she started breathing again everything was OK."[2]

Dr. Laura noticed me, and she refused to let me fall to the bottom of my own pool of sorrow.

I understood now what it meant to receive help. It doesn't make someone weak if they are drowning—they just need support to start breathing again.

TO CONTEMPLATE

When someone brings out their phone to take a picture of you, what thoughts race through your mind about how you might appear? For so long I hid my teeth when people would tell me to smile for photos. Is there anything about yourself you try to hide while being seen? Can you consider why this might be?

SELF-PORTRAIT PROMPT

Create an image that shows the embrace of self with imperfections on display and honored.

Find a way to feel movement and joy for yourself and document the good endorphins running through you in a picture. For example, an unrestrained dance party is my go-to for getting my body into a place where I'm able to freely express, whether it's laughter and joy or sadness and anger. Let whatever needs to surface come up and move through you. Do not think about how your smile or your body looks. Just let yourself feel the joy without looking to limit its expression.

THE GIFT OF OUR FAULTS

I'd been trying to escape
earthquakes all my life—
I ceased being afraid
when I stopped all the running.

I faced the broken earth,
knelt down with empathy,
and traced my fault lines
as a map of discovery.

I rested my cheek gently
on my hyper-pulsing heart,
provided water to my parched landscapes,
and held my own hand to travel the uncharted
 distance of the deep.

I realized this is what my father could never do—
see his fault lines as a gift.

Now I wear my imperfections proudly for us both—
not as paying a penance or carrying a curse,
but as the shining badge of being human.
Not broken like a *problem to be fixed*,
but a glorious person just longing to be loved.

CHAPTER 10

ATTUNING TO THE FREQUENCY OF LOVE

If you don't become the ocean, you'll be seasick every day.
Leonard Cohen

One of the last things I remember my father saying to me when I was a young teen was that he wished he had never given me the name Joy. That I wasn't anything like who he'd hoped I would become.

That was the point when I set a serious boundary and completely cut off communication with him. Looking back, I now realize that *he* was the one who wasn't capable of embodying joy and was just projecting that onto me.

Throughout those years of abandonment, whenever his birthday inevitably rolled around, I'd just try to stay busy and ignore it. But after almost thirty years, as his seventieth was coming up, I found something that inspired a shift. While my family and I were packing up to move across the country, my mom pulled some important paperwork from her lockbox for me to take with me. There was a copy of my birth certificate, medical records, drawings from when I was little, and a term paper I had written for my Intro to Psychology class in my freshman year of college. I had titled the paper "The Psychological Effects on Daughters Emotionally Abused by Their Fathers."

Just . . . whoa. Eighteen-year-old Joy was brave. The paper was thorough and informative, and my teen self had gone way above and beyond on the length and content. It was obvious that I had used the assignment as an opportunity to study and try to solve myself. I remember how deeply validating it was, when doing all that psych research, to finally name the abuse that had changed the structure of my brain. I could see from an objective source how I, my mom, and my brother all suffered the effects of traumatizing manipulation, invalidation, gaslighting, neglect, and toxic enmeshment. The thing is, I could also feel the anger permeating my written words. Looking back now, I see how that anger kept me in resentment for so, so long.

The final portion of my term paper had a detailed plan for how my future self could go about completing the healing process I had laid out based on research from experts and psychologists. Here's what I wrote:

> First comes anger and then when you accept the pain come the tears which are transformational and bring compassion into the heart of the wounded daughter. And then, she must, on a personal level, redeem her father to herself. This is the most difficult part of healing, but the most important. Even if the father is no longer in the picture, it is the inward father and the daughter's relationship that still needs to be transformed. If this doesn't happen the old patterns will continue. The daughter

must come to find value in her father, because if she doesn't, the parts of her that resemble him in her mind will remain unintegrated and potentially destructive.

I barely remembered writing that paper, but it was like I had foreseen the future and what my life would hold. It was amazing, heartbreaking, and overwhelming. For so many years I had wondered why I felt emotionally stuck. Why trying to accept myself had felt impossible and loving others felt so complicated.

My younger self really knocked it out of the park with this next mic drop of an honest confession: "For me, I am not yet to the point where I can look in the mirror and be okay with seeing the struggles my father has imposed upon me reflected back. Seeing him in me means I have his shadow which is dark and terrifying."

I never wanted to be like him. I had run away from any part of me that resembled him—or thought I had. The thing is that the self-abandonment had been internalized very early on. So this next admission from Teen Me really lit a fire beneath me as I read it again twenty-six years later:

> I accept that by rejecting my father, I am refusing my power because in rejecting him I am rejecting all his positive qualities with the negative. I'm not valuing myself for what I have to offer. But for now, though, I am still struggling with coming to terms with breaking down my protective shell. This will prove to be a lifelong process I will be dealing with. The comfort in all of this is that I can now look forward to the day that I can look into the mirror and have the strength to just smile.

I took the pen I was holding while reading the term paper and wrote a note to myself right next to those words of hope:

> "Forgiveness means releasing our rage and our need to retaliate. ... It is an act of letting go so that we ourselves can go on."
>
> —Sue Monk Kidd

Well, Little Joy, Mama Joy is here now, and we are about to reclaim our power!

I felt so proud of myself for doing the work and becoming the woman who could fulfill my own prophecy.

Author Sue Monk Kidd writes, "Forgiveness means releasing our rage and our need to retaliate, no longer dwelling on the offense, the offender, and the suffering, and rising to a higher love. It is an act of letting go so that we ourselves can go on."[1] To find my power, I had to identify the parts of my father that were also part of me. I had to realize how my father took on victimhood as his complete identity. I think it took me a long time to see it that way because I had so much empathy for his sorrow. I just assumed that his victimhood was inherent—I didn't know that it could also be a choice. Because he had told me that he couldn't escape being a victim, I also believed that to be true about myself.

I spent my childhood internalizing the belief that I was and would always be a helpless victim. I then spent a decade of my marriage pushing back against my husband, unconsciously justifying my victim identity as the reason I deserved more grace than he did. He'd always tell me that I never listened to him, which I just took to mean that he didn't really understand me, but unconsciously I'd been repeating the pattern of communication that my dad passed on to me.

After I began doing the work of unlearning toxic belief patterns, it finally clicked that my husband was correct—I never really was hearing him. I was too focused on being offended and didn't know how to meet in the middle and collectively grow to move forward. No one had ever modeled for me how to resolve conflict in a healing way. I never saw my father ever back down from his commitment to rightness, and I had learned to do the same. I was a very good soldier in the army of rightness—but I no longer wanted to harm those I was in relationship with or hurt myself. The dissonance clanged like an energetic cymbal beneath my skin—desperation to experience unrestrained freedom apart from my programmed self.

I didn't want to be in a defensive posture anymore. I no longer cared about being right. I just wanted to be gentle, to be at peace, to embody love. I realized that, even though intellectually I believed that I wanted to break the generational curse of emotional invalidation and the posture of control, I had to learn to embody those beliefs.

What if, instead of punishing ourselves for not being someone else's version of perfect, we could give ourselves permission to live freely and wonderfully *flawed*?

One of my favorite books is *A Wrinkle in Time* by Madeleine L'Engle. It's the story of a girl named Meg who is searching through space and time to find her father, who has gotten lost in the dark confusion of his own mind's journey. Ultimately, Meg's passion and conviction are what save him, but only as she uses the divine gifts given to her by Mrs Who, Mrs Which, and Mrs Whatsit, three supernatural beings who are sort of like fairy godmothers and help guide her.

In a powerful scene, as Meg is preparing to fight the darkness of Camazotz, a planet known for its pure evil, Mrs Whatsit says, "Meg, I give you your faults."

"My faults!" Meg cried.

"Your faults."

"But I'm always trying to get rid of my faults!"

"Yes," Mrs Whatsit said. "However, I think you'll find they'll come in very handy on Camazotz."[2]

That image of Meg's faults as a tool of empowerment stayed with me. Recognizing and vulnerably naming her imperfections out loud is what gave her the energy she needed to push back against the darkness, and embracing what she believed to be her greatest weaknesses was the secret key to resurrection. Learning to do this for myself has been the way to move from victimhood to trailblazing.

I began to contemplate anything good I remembered about my father that I might have blocked out or forgotten in the years since our relationship was severed. I remembered that he had been a competitive swimmer from childhood up through college, but I didn't have any memories of him playing with me in the pool or even swimming on his own. My mom had told me he loved swimming more than anything but took it so seriously that any imperfection in his performance would upset him for weeks.

In an effort to reclaim my power and redeem my internal father to myself, I decided to commemorate my father's upcoming seventieth birthday by swimming. I made my first ever appointment at the local community pool and committed myself to the belief that if I could confront and embrace the parts of me that were like him, I could heal.

It was still dark outside when I pulled into the parking lot of the community pool at 6:54 a.m. on his birthday. I sat there in the driver's seat for six long minutes of self-criticism. I thought of every excuse not to go in.

This is stupid—one time of swimming is not going to heal you.

You don't know what you're doing, and you'll be a burden to the real swimmers.

The water will probably be cold.

You didn't bring the right sandals.

There's no use trying—you're going to be broken forever.
You are too late to redeem anything.
Just move on already—what's the point?

My subconscious was really trying to protect me from the potential danger of change.

Right then my phone buzzed on the passenger seat with a text notification—*a distraction from my negative thoughts.* I picked it up and looked. It was from Carrie, my alchemizing friend:

> Good morning, Joy. I've been thinking about our time shared together after my mastectomy and I have no words, only tears, to express the gratitude that you came to sit vigil with me and capture the most vulnerable and important moments of the intense beauty that were the sacred days following my surgery. The magic of those days has passed, but as I ponder (and ponder, and ponder) these images, the cloud settles in around me again; the holy made present here and now. The pictures are reinvigorating my heart in places where it has died. You are so very dear to me.

Of course, I was weeping and could barely see through the tears to read the screen. I responded instantly in gratitude. I told her that I was sitting in the parking lot of the lap pool on the brink of my own metamorphosis. I told her that I felt frozen in the car and terrified to face whatever I was about to encounter in that water.

She texted back:

> I am so proud of you for staring this straight in the eyes. It means stretching one tip of your wing into the burning sensation of the actual sun, when all you've known is fabricated light. And tomorrow stretching it one centimeter further. Giving yourself over to the burning sensation, and the relief of it stopping once you pull back when it becomes too much. And

before you know it, you're fully out in the sun. And once that kind of authentic Light shines on you, there's nothing that can shut down the instincts that point you to true north. You are becoming you.

I double-tapped that text message six or seven times and took three different screenshots. Those words from Carrie are as precious to me as pictures of my kids when they were babies. She was infusing me with her golden wisdom on how to shine.

It seems that maybe we all begin in the darkness, and as we slowly, vulnerably acclimate to the honest feeling of light, we close the gap between who we think we are supposed to be and who we actually *are*.

Our radiant power is already in us—we just have to *claim it*.

I took a big, huge breath and forced myself to go into the community center. I pushed through the glass doors and walked up to the check-in counter. A woman with kind eyes looked up at me and immediately said, "Well, hello! Aren't you an *early* bird?!" And, well, that was all it took to start me crying. I didn't know how much I had been believing that I was just too late to heal my wounds. But I was not too late. In fact, I was right on time.

She noticed I had tears and said, "Oh no, I'm so sorry! Did I say something wrong? And . . . I haven't seen you before, is this your first time at the pool?"

I looked up and reassured her that she'd done nothing to upset me. "It's just," I hesitated, not sure if I was feeling too tender to tell her my real reason for being there that day. I uttered, "Well, my father was a competitive swimmer. And today is his birthday, and, well, I wanted to honor that and swim."

Upon hearing that, she began crying—quite loudly, in fact—and called to her partner, "Todd! Come over here and listen to this story of how she's swimming to honor her father who was a competitive swimmer and passed away and today

is his birthday! Isn't that the most beautiful thing?" At which point Todd came over and echoed her emotional display of pride for me, and I just couldn't squash their special moment. I chuckled inwardly, and I felt deep in my spirit that this "accidental" misunderstanding about my dad being dead was far from an accident.

This was an opportunity to tell myself a new story about my father. I didn't necessarily have to think or say he was dead, but maybe I could stop repeating that I had been *abandoned*. Maybe one of the gifts that came from visiting the pool was finding a fresh perspective on who I am as daughter. All my life I'd been trying to figure out what I had done wrong to be so unlovable that my own father would choose to turn away from me. Now, I could release the need to figure that out.

There was nothing else left to figure. All that was left to do was jump into the pool.

I put my clothes in the locker room, tied up my hair, put on my brand-new swim cap and goggles, and walked down the hall toward the thick aroma of chlorine. My body tensed up a bit, worried that I might not know the correct swimming etiquette or which lane to swim in or stay in. I started to get in my head. That is, until I saw the pool—it was completely open. Of all eight spots that could have been booked, I was the only one.

Todd walked in to pick up some towels. "Lookie there, that rarely happens! Special just for your dad's birthday swim, I guess. You could have fun and be like a dolphin and leap over all the lane dividers!" And then he was gone. I tell ya, it was as though God's voice of love was feeding these people a script.

I had been so worried about not doing the whole swimming thing right. Worried about being too late to heal. Yet, there I stood, with a room the size of a movie theater all to myself. With windows for a ceiling and murals of happy orcas painted on the walls. With no chance I could do it wrong and no timeline I had missed.

I gripped the metal handrail and stepped down into the shallow end of the pool. It was a wonderful kind of unexpected warmth that reminded me instantly of stepping into the birthing pool Donny had filled with water just before I birthed our son Smith at home. All I know is that even though I had never been in that pool before, the water felt familiar. I splashed my feet around a little and tried to focus on why I had wanted to be there right then, right there, on that day.

I wanted to choose loving myself over hating myself.

To love myself, I had to find a way to accept the parts of me that were like my father, who I had previously named as bad. To endear myself to him, I had to get close to those parts I didn't fully understand. Instead of shaming him, I had to try to get to know him. I was determined to get to know the true him, the childlike him, beneath all of the fear and trauma and regret—the him that once came alive in the water.

I dove in fully. I leaped over the lane dividers like a freaking dolphin. I cried. I laughed. I played. I flipped onto my back and let the water cradle me without restraint. While I floated on my back, watching the light sparkling and reflecting off the windows, all I felt was immense gratitude. I closed my eyes, filled my lungs with air, and let myself be lifted by the water. It was at that moment that the recognizable sound of Alanis Morrisette's song "You Learn" came blaring in from the boxing gym next door.

"I recommend getting your heart trampled on . . ."

I instantly full-body laughed out loud in surprise and delight.

I mean, *of course* it was Alanis. Her album *Jagged Little Pill* was released the year that my mom finally left my dad and filed for divorce. I would scream Alanis's music at full volume to feel emotional release. She was my queen, my midwife of emotional expression, and my teen-angst raging companion. Now, here she was with me again, on the other side of that anger. She was delivering a holy message through her gravelly, give-it-all-you-got melody "You Learn."

It was *the* song for *that* moment. I had loved and bled and learned and screamed and worn myself out and melted it all down. And I imagine that if you've made it this far into the book, at one time you too have found yourself singing along to a similar soundtrack.

There's no doubt these melodies help carry us across our thresholds of identity where we move from constriction into expanse. It's like Richard Rohr writes,

> We have to allow ourselves to be drawn into sacred space, into liminality. All transformation takes place here. We have to allow

ourselves to be drawn out of "business as usual" and remain patiently on the "threshold" where we are betwixt and between the familiar and the completely unknown. There alone is our old world left behind, while we are not yet sure of the new existence. That's a good space where genuine newness can begin.³

Leaving the community pool that day after my swim, the woman with kind eyes behind the desk called after me as I pushed the exterior door open, "See you soon! And what's your name, hon?"

"It's Joy," I told her.

"Oh *yes*! Of course, that's *exactly* who you are!"

I felt it right in the heart.

She was right—I was Joy, and I could claim me as my own.

The water offered me the gift of seeing myself from a new perspective, an image of myself with an undefended heart. Hear me loud and clear, friend: Even through the rocky waves and daunting depths, in our practice of self-compassion we *can* still come to see ourselves with a kind of clarity.

Swimming has been one way I have learned to sing *my* healing song of alchemy—along with the portraits I have taken of myself all throughout the journey.

With each intention to befriend our own darkness, we melt down self-hatred into self-love. Compassion for our deepest aches comes when we dive into the deep ocean of *not knowing*. It is a falling away from the need for everything to make sense, the need to be right, the belief that everything must be done perfectly, and the need to save everyone from everything.

Instead of turning outward for proof that we are worthy of compassion, we learn to turn *inward*. It's there we see that our feeling of seasickness is, in reality, homesickness.

We are not washed up or unworthy or irrevocably wounded— we are only longing to uncover the home within *ourselves*.

TO CONTEMPLATE

What could it look like for you to redeem parts of your story to yourself, even if the people involved in your story are no longer a part of your life? What parts of your life might be resolved outwardly but still need to be redeemed inwardly?

SELF-PORTRAIT PROMPT

Create an image that is symbolic of the resurrection of your personal superpower of compassion.

For example, if it is the rebirth of your original childlike goodness, it could be a photograph of you in motion: swinging high in the air on a swing, lying down and rolling around in the grass, or blowing a dandelion flower and watching the tiny seeds float in the light.

Consider how you might create an image that shows your empathetic embrace and attunement with all the previous versions of yourself.

A REFUSAL EVER TO GO NUMB AGAIN

"How do I become an octopus?"
(I had to figure it out . . .)
One arm to cook,
One arm to clean,
One arm to provide.
One to affix my smile,
One extended as partner,
One soothing the babies,
One easing the ache in my teens,
One arm to hold myself as I hold them,
One arm, one arm—
and I realized . . .
not even an octopus
has enough limbs to do it all,
to hold it all.
So I released it all completely,
and learned that an octopus spends their whole existence
SEEKING TO HIDE.

Covering themselves to protect all that is vulnerable with
 their ever-extended arms.
They become camouflage—
and I no longer care to be hidden.
In a rush of courage, I abandoned figuring it all out
and embraced humanity instead.
Just one vulnerably wide-open heart,
two imperfectly loving flailing arms,
and a refusal to ever go numb again
in the depths
of the sea.

ACKNOWLEDGMENTS

Fisher: You have been my greatest teacher in the art of self-compassion. Thank you for your curiosity and your courage.

Donny: The words in this book are mine, but the time to create them was only possible because of your willingness to carry everything else. Thank you.

Mom: Thank you for praying for me every day of my life and for modeling how to believe in growth, even when it was slow, even in the darkest seasons. Through all those years that I resisted the light, you still showed me how to face the sun. Thank you. Thank you. Thank you.

To my kids: Thank you for celebrating me every step of the way. You are each a miracle.

Tommy: Okay, soulmate, tag you're it . . . your turn to start writing. I will be your #1 fan always.

Sharyn and Chip: Your belief in my words, even when they were a mess of confusion, has been the fire keeping me warm as I've become an author. Thank you for not invalidating my expression and for unconditionally loving me—all the versions of myself I have ever been.

Gwen: You are a trailblazer of the heart, an ally to the exhausted and overwhelmed, and a book doula. Thank you for holding my words and my imperfect being with tenderness and power.

Ali: You are the Priestess, never forget. You've accompanied me through the journey of each of these words as they grew in both of our hearts. Thank you for never giving up on me and for being my person, my encourager, and the one to bring me a lantern when I retreat into my cave.

Kim: You are the Auntie I never knew my children needed. Thank you for giving all of us the courage to become allies, your friends, your family. You have helped me learn how to love well, and this is only the beginning. Your beautifully expanding self is breathtaking—thank you for letting me be your witness.

Rachel: You have modeled for me that, to quote Joy Sullivan, "joy is not a trick." Thank you for showing me how to plant marigolds in the garden of my own life and how to revel in the beauty.

Chrystal: My sister, you've been my family. Thank you for your commitment to keep finding me in my isolation. Your belief in the value of village is pure gospel goodness. Never give up (unless you want to, and if you do, I will meet you at the lazy river with a margarita and solidarity).

Ash: You are the rainbow angel in the painting my Mabel created. Keep singing your heavenly song.

Cere: Your radiance is contagious. Thank you for welcoming me and my family into your arms. Your beautiful and soul-nourishing homemade bread sustained me as I wrote. Thank you for allowing me to bear witness to your unbelievable courage in the face of incomprehensible heartbreak. I love you.

Vida: Your presence has taught me the expansiveness of God's love and I will never be the same. Thank you for opening the portal of divine mystery and guiding me into the beauty of your island.

Nicole, Jarrod, and kids: You are the bravest family I have ever known. I pray your vulnerability lays the foundation for what we all hope the church can someday become. You are beloved.

Carrie: You are a golden butterfly of miraculous grace. How did I get so lucky to call you friend? Thank you for your stunningly glorious words of honesty in all of those moments I found myself questioning my own worthiness of being seen. I love you in the marrow of my bones.

K.J.: I can't remember a time when I felt more in the obvious presence of God's love than when I was with you in your backyard, witnessing your beautiful acceptance of self. Thank you for seeing me in a way that others never will. Thank you for reminding me of the pure gospel message in your companionship.

Misha: Thank you for the gift of seeing me fully and helping me to see myself as an evolving, blooming flower (just as lovely and meaningful in winter as in the summer). I could not be more grateful that I answered the call of Beauty that led me straight to your magical garden gate.

Joy (my agent): Your encouragement has been oxygen to my weary fingers on the keyboard. Thank you for not letting me snuff out the fire.

The team at Baker Books: Thank you for believing in this book, guiding its journey, and opening up space for hard questions to be asked and embraced in expansive love.

NOTES

Chapter 1 Discovering a Perspective of Empathy

1. Frank Boreman, "Earthrise: What It's Like to Escape Our Planet | Op-Docs" (video), *New York Times*, October 5, 2018, 1:27 to 1:40, https://www.youtube.com/watch?v=syQi7Q-ITCE.

2. Richard Goldstein, "William A. Anders, 90, Dies; Flew on First Manned Orbit of the Moon," *New York Times*, June 7, 2024, https://www.nytimes.com/2024/06/07/science/william-a-anders-dead.html.

3. Bill Nelson (@SenBillNelson), "He traveled to the threshold of the Moon," X, June 7, 2024, https://x.com/SenBillNelson/status/1799246936937300465.

4. Jim Clash, "Astronaut Bill Anders Recalls Famous 'Earthrise' Photo He Took from Moon," *Forbes*, April 17, 2015, https://www.forbes.com/sites/jimclash/2015/04/17/bill-anders-recalls-famous-earthrise-photo-he-took-from-moon/.

Chapter 2 Answering the Call of Beauty

1. Liz Milani, "Beauty Beyond Standards, Part 4," The Practice Co., accessed February 21, 2024, https://www.thepracticeco.com/.

2. Emma Seppala, "The Scientific Benefits of Self-Compassion," The Center for Compassion and Altruism Research and Education, May 8, 2014, https://ccare.stanford.edu/uncategorized/the-scientific-benefits-of-self-compassion-infographic/.

3. John O'Donohue, *Divine Beauty: The Invisible Embrace* (Bantam, 2004), 7.

4. O'Donohue, *Divine Beauty*, 7.

5. "Recognizing Burnout and Finding Our Way Back to Self with Natalie Kuhn," *justUS* (podcast), June 17, 2024, https://www.justuspodcast.com/episodes/recognizing-burnout-and-finding-our-way-back-to-self-with-natalie-kuhn.

6. *NYAD*, directed by Elizabeth Chai Vasarhelyi and Jimmy Chin (Netflix, 2023).

Chapter 3 Contemplation That Leads to Transformation

1. Frank White, *The Overview Effect: Space Exploration and Human Evolution*, 2nd ed. (American Institute of Aeronautics and Astronautics, 1998).
2. Nicole Scott, *Back to Earth: What Life in Space Taught Me About Our Home Planet—And Our Mission to Protect It* (Seal Press, 2021).
3. William James, *The Varieties of Religious Experience: A Study in Human Nature* (Longmans, Green & Co, 1902).
4. Steven Stolper, "The Refrigerator Tree," NatureOutside, October 12, 2016, https://www.natureoutside.com/the-refrigerator-tree/.
5. Katherine May, *Wintering: The Power of Rest and Retreat in Difficult Times* (Riverhead Books, 2020), 14.
6. Britannica Dictionary Online, under "crucible," accessed February 11, 2025, https://www.britannica.com/dictionary/crucible.

Chapter 4 Validating Emotion

1. Elizabeth Barrett Browning, *Aurora Leigh: A Poem in Nine Books* (1856; repr., T. Y. Crowell & Co., 1883), 265.
2. Becky Kennedy (@drbeckyatgoodinside), "Validate before you understand," Instagram, November 6, 2022, https://www.instagram.com/reel/Cko5h06BxTw/?igsh=dDRmN2FwNWJuc2Qy.

Chapter 5 Embodying Authenticity

1. Laura E. Anderson, *When Religion Hurts You: Healing from Religious Trauma and the Impact of High-Control Religion* (Brazos Press, 2023), 43.
2. Anderson, *When Religion Hurts You*, 44.
3. Anderson, *When Religion Hurts You*, 44.
4. Martha Beck, *The Way of Integrity* (Random House, 2021), xxii.
5. Elizabeth Gilbert, *Big Magic: Creative Living Beyond Fear* (Random House, 2015), 9.
6. Thanks to author, speaker, and leadership coach Jo Saxton for this insightful question.

Chapter 6 Moving from Criticism to Curiosity

1. Harry Cloke, "The Science Behind Curiosity in Learning," May 2023, https://www.growthengineering.co.uk/what-is-curiosity/.
2. Marie Forleo, *Everything Is Figureoutable* (Portfolio, 2019), 75.
3. Flynn Skidmore (@flynnskidmore), "There are two versions of self-awareness," TikTok, January 7, 2024, https://www.tiktok.com/@flynn.skidmore/video/7321539999466327338.
4. Skidmore, "There are two versions of self-awareness."
5. Jon Kabat-Zinn, "It's not a matter of letting go," Facebook, November 5, 2023, https://www.facebook.com/kabatzinn/posts/its-not

-a-matter-of-letting-go-you-would-if-you-could-instead-of-let-it-go-we-sh/863346205159872/.

6. Louise Hay, *You Can Heal Your Life* (Hay House, 1984), 20.

7. "What Is Internal Family Systems?," IFS Institute, accessed June 24, 2024, https://ifs-institute.com.

8. Richard Rohr, "An Unspeakable Name," Center for Action and Contemplation, September 21, 2020, https://cac.org/daily-meditations/an-unspeakable-name-2020-09-21/.

Chapter 7 Claiming Wholeness

1. Liz Milani, "Everyday Alchemy: Transmuting Challenges into Opportunities," The Practice Co., accessed February 21, 2024, https://www.thepracticeco.com/.

2. Milani, "Everyday Alchemy."

3. "Joan Didion: Crafting an Elegy for Her Daughter," *Fresh Air*, November 2, 2011, https://www.npr.org/transcripts/141808816.

4. Richard Rohr, "Liminal Space," Center for Action and Contemplation, July 7, 2016, https://cac.org/daily-meditations/liminal-space-2016-07-07/.

5. Jason Morriss, sermon at Austin New Church, January 21, 2024, 31:10 to 31:35, https://www.youtube.com/watch?v=IQqMlpmkrkQ.

Chapter 8 Releasing the Weight of Shame

1. *Jerry Maguire*, directed by Cameron Crowe (TriStar Pictures, 1996).

Chapter 9 Embracing Joy

1. Quoted in Parker Palmer, *Let Your Life Speak: Listening for the Voice of Vocation* (Jossey-Bass, 1999), 19.

2. Esther Addley, "Dramatic Rescue at World Championships After Swimmer Faints and Sinks to Bottom of Pool," *The Guardian*, June 23, 2022, https://www.theguardian.com/sport/2022/jun/23/dramatic-rescue-at-world-championships-after-swimmer-faints-and-sinks-to-bottom-of-pool.

Chapter 10 Attuning to the Frequency of Love

1. Sue Monk Kidd, *The Dance of the Dissident Daughter: A Woman's Journey from Christian Tradition to the Sacred Feminine* (HarperOne, 2016), 221.

2. Madeleine L'Engle, *A Wrinkle in Time* (Square Fish, 1962), 112.

3. Rohr, "Liminal Space."

JOY PROUTY is a professional photographer, filmmaker, poet, creative strategist, and mentor to artists. Through workshops and online experiences, Joy teaches empathetic visual storytelling and self-validation through creativity. Her work has been featured in a wide variety of print and entertainment media worldwide. Joy lives on a tiny, magical, and mossy island in the Pacific Northwest with her partner, Donny, and their seven children.

CONNECT WITH JOY

www.JoyProuty.com

 @joyprouty